SO-EIG-184

The Inside Scoop on . . .

Home Plate Umpires

Kirk Gibson of the Tigers learned all about expanding strike zones as a rookie. "During one game that was dragging on and on, the ump told me he had a plane to catch and that I'd better be swinging—and not only at things that were close. He wasn't kidding because I was out of there real quick."

Pitchers' Psych Out Games

Charlie Kerfeld of the Astros makes himself look like a slob so batters will underestimate him. "I spit [tobacco juice] all over myself. When I come into a game, batters say, 'Hey, look at that hog with spit all over him. He can't get anybody out.' That's what I want them to think."

Bullpen Shenanigans

Dave Stewart of the Athletics developed a game he calls "Master Pain." It's to see which player in the bullpen can stand the most pain. "You sit there and pull hairs out of each other's nose. Is that wacky enough for you?"

Batting Slumps

"When I struggle at the plate," says Ozzie Guillen of the White Sox, "I ask the trainer for eye drops and I put them right on my bat so my bat can see the ball good."

And Much More, in . . .
Baseball Confidential™

Books by Bruce Nash and Allan Zullo

The Baseball Hall of Shame™
The Baseball Hall of Shame 2™
The Baseball Hall of Shame 3™
The Football Hall of Shame™
The Sports Hall of Shame™
Baseball Confidential™
The Misfortune 500™

Published by POCKET BOOKS

Most Pocket Books are available at special quantity discounts for bulk purchases for sales promotions, premiums or fund raising. Special books or book excerpts can also be created to fit specific needs.

For details write the office of the Vice President of Special Markets, Pocket Books, 1230 Avenue of the Americas, New York, New York 10020.

BASEBALL CONFIDENTIAL™

BRUCE NASH
and
ALLAN ZULLO

POCKET BOOKS

New York   London   Toronto   Sydney   Tokyo

Several players have changed teams since the *Baseball
Confidential* survey was conducted in the summer of 1987.
Throughout this book, we identify players with the teams they
played for at the time they took part in the survey.

An *Original* publication of POCKET BOOKS

POCKET BOOKS, a division of Simon & Schuster, Inc.,
1230 Avenue of the Americas, New York, N.Y. 10020

Copyright © 1988 by Nash and Zullo Productions, Inc.
Cover artwork copyright © 1988 by Joseph Csatari

Baseball Confidential is a trademark
of Nash and Zullo Productions, Inc.

All rights reserved, including the right to reproduce
this book or portions thereof in any form whatsoever.
For information address Pocket Books,
1230 Avenue of the Americas, New York, N.Y. 10020

ISBN: 0-671-69217-8

First Pocket Books trade paperback printing April, 1988

10 9 8 7 6 5 4 3

POCKET and colophon are trademarks of
Simon & Schuster, Inc.

Printed in U.S.A.

DEDICATION

In loving memory of Sophie and John Mitchell for blessing me with such a wonderful wife.

B.N.

To David Wartowski, Shawn Barbagallo, Adam Holt, and Frankie Linquist, with hopes they'll grow up to be great sports—and great ball players.

A.Z.

CONTENTS

ACKNOWLEDGMENT

We wish to thank the more than 200 major league players, managers, coaches, and general managers who graciously consented to participate in the *Baseball Confidential* survey.

We are especially grateful to the team of beat reporters who so professionally carried out our survey: Bill Althaus, *The Examiner,* Independence, Missouri; Barry Bloom, *The Tribune,* San Diego; Bill Brown, *Delaware County Daily Times,* Pennsylvania; Steve Buckley, *The Tacoma News Tribune;* Nick Cafardo, *The Patriot Ledger,* Quincy, Massachusetts; Tony DeMarco, *Fort Worth Star-Telegram;* Tom Flaherty, *The Milwaukee Journal;* Bud Geracie, *Mercury-News,* San Jose, California; Wesley Goldstein, Canadian Press, Montreal Bureau; Bob Hertzel, *The Pittsburgh Press;* Greg Hoard, *The Cincinnati Enquirer;* Neil Hohlfeld, *Houston Chronicle;* Rick Hummel, *St. Louis Post-Dispatch;* Bruce Levine, Chicago Sports Tapes, Inc.; Frank McLean, CKOC Radio, Hamilton, Ontario, Canada; Fred Mitchell, *Chicago Tribune;* Tom Pedulla, Gannett Newspapers, New York; Mike Peticca, Associated Press, Cleveland Bureau; Vern Plagenhoef, Booth Newspapers, Michigan; Peter Schmuck, *The Register,* Orange County, California; Larry Schwartz, *The Record,* Hackensack, New Jersey; Melody Simmons, *The Evening Sun,* Baltimore; Claire Smith, *The Hartford Courant;* Joe Strauss, *Columbus Ledger-Enquirer,* Georgia, and Gregg Wong, *St. Paul Pioneer Press.* We also wish to thank Gerry Fraley, president of the Baseball Writers Association of America.

For their fine work in transcribing hundreds of hours of tapes, we extend our appreciation to: Alena Bybee, Janice Callahan, Laurel Coker, Jim DeEduardo, B. J. Dixon, Pamela Gray, Cynthia Kratz, Jennifer Laur, Lana Thompson, and Janine Sherry.

For their understanding, patience, and help, we thank Sophie, Robyn, and Jennifer Nash; Kathy, Allison, and Sasha Zullo; and Eleanor Arnold.

CONFIDENTIALLY SPEAKING

In our travels across the country researching offbeat sports stories for books and television specials, fans have asked us some intriguing questions about baseball. How do relief pitchers pass the time in the bullpen? What players conduct the most bizarre pregame rituals? What is *really* said during conferences on the mound? How do batters psyche out pitchers? What sneaky ruses do players use to avoid signing autographs?

We didn't know the answers. So we decided to find out. Because so many fans wanted to know more about baseball than what they'd seen on TV or from the grandstands, we set out to conduct a comprehensive, never-before-attempted survey of major league baseball. Our goal was to uncover the inside scoop—from the gossipy to the screwy, from the inspiring to the fascinating—about our national pastime.

First, we needed to find out more of the questions fans wanted answered. During spring training in 1987, we visited Grapefruit League ball parks and asked fans for the questions they wanted to ask major leaguers. After listening to hundreds of fans, we selected a slate of questions for an in-depth survey designed to reveal the behind-the-scenes lowdown about life in the bigs.

We then assembled a crack team of 26 reporters, each one a professional who covers a major league club for a newspaper or radio station. Armed with the survey, these reporters questioned players in clubhouses before and after games, on team flights, and in hotel lobbies. During the summer of 1987, 208 major leaguers took part in this unique survey—from superstars like Dave Winfield and Wade Boggs to rookies like Kevin Seitzer and Billy Ripkin; from managers like Whitey Herzog and Sparky Anderson to All-Stars like Ryne Sandberg and Tony Gwynn. Complementing the players' responses, coaches, general managers, and beat reporters—those who know the players best—were also polled.

The players knew that their answers were being taped for the record unless they requested that their names be withheld on certain answers. Fortunately, the overwhelming majority of answers in the book are attributed because the players got into the spirit of this unprecedented, off-the-wall survey.

While most players took the survey in good humor, others rejected it out of hand. George Brett of the Royals had so much fun answering the questions that he returned the next day to elaborate on his responses. Not so Reggie Jackson of the Athletics. He made it perfectly clear he wanted nothing to do with the survey. That prompted teammate Bill Caudill, who participated in the survey, to joke, "That's good. That means my stuff has a better chance of getting into the book." Echoing the view shared by many players, veteran Bill Madlock of the Tigers said, "Some of these questions are hard, maybe because I've never been asked them before."

Because we didn't want to turn off the players and jeopardize the survey, we did not include questions about their sex life or drugs. However, we did probe the players' nightlives by asking these survey questions: "What players have the reputation for being ladies' men?" and "What players like to party into the wee hours of the morning?" We shouldn't have bothered. These were the only two questions major leaguers considered much too sensitive to answer—even anonymously.

But the answers they did give filled hundreds of hours of tapes which took weeks for a team of typists to transcribe. Then we sifted through thousands of answers as we compiled the survey's outrageous results. We included as many unedited player comments as possible—when you read them, you can actually "hear" the players speak.

The chapters of *Baseball Confidential* are structured to give you the feeling that you are opening a door to the inner world of baseball. We want you to get an insider's view of the game from every vantage point possible—beyond the box scores and statistical analyses. This book will take you into the clubhouse, the dugout, and the bullpen. At times, you may even end up way out in left field!

HOME PLATE

**WHICH CATCHERS ARE BEST
AT RATTLING BATTERS?**

1. **Tony Peña**
2. **Gary Carter**
3. **Carlton Fisk**
4. **Mike Heath**
5. **Mike LaValliere**

Hitting requires a great deal of concentration, so most catchers do whatever they can to distract the batter. Usually, it's as simple as striking up a seemingly innocent conversation. But some backstoppers have gone to extremes and told hitters what pitch is coming.

Brewers veteran outfielder Rick Manning says he's amazed at how well the pitch-calling ploy works. If the catcher tips the batter off to the first few pitches, "you don't know what to think, whether he's telling the truth or not on the next pitch," said Manning. "Personally, I try to ignore it."

Phillies catcher Darren Daulton admits sometimes telling the batter what pitch is coming. "One time we were facing a hitter who was wearing us out, so I started telling him what was coming. It messed with his mind and we got him out. I've done that a few times to others and it's worked except once when the guy got a base hit up the middle."

Bruce Benedict of the Braves once tipped off Padres hitting star Tony Gwynn. Recalled Gwynn: "One night when Bruce was behind the plate, I was three for three and had tagged the ball hard every time. As I came to the plate for the fourth time, Bruce turned to me and said, 'Tony, I'm going to have the pitcher throw it right down the middle. Let's see what you can do with it.' I didn't believe him. Sure enough, the pitcher threw the ball right down the middle for strike one. Bruce said, 'Okay, I'm going to call a curve inside this time.' The pitcher threw a curve. I hit a ground ball and made an out. So the fifth time I came up to the plate, I asked Bruce, 'Why are you telling me what pitches are coming?' And he said, 'Because we can't get you out any other way. I figure if I tell you what's coming, maybe you'll get yourself out.' "

Sometimes catchers deliberately try to annoy batters. Athletics catcher Mickey Tettleton says he likes to throw dirt on the shoes of batters he knows personally just to get a little rise out of them.

Cardinals catcher Tony Peña takes the irritation factor a step further, said Expos outfielder Herm Winningham. "I stepped into the batter's box and was waiting for the pitch when all of a sudden, he spit on my shoe. I took the pitch and then stepped out of the box and told Tony, 'If you do that again, I'll beat you with this bat.' I didn't really mean it, but I had to say something back. Of course, he did what he set out to do. He broke my concentration."

Peña, whom players say is the biggest chatterbox in the National League, usually relies on the most common form of batter-rattling—small talk.

"Some catchers try to mess up your mind," says Yankees star Dave Winfield. "Guys like Mike Heath [of the Tigers] and Carlton Fisk [of the White Sox] talk a lot. I used to have to tell Heath to shut up. I don't want to hear any of that. Fisk is always talking to batters, crying about his aches and pains or his bad swing. Catchers like that are just looking for ways to get me out because they know I'll do some damage."

Pirates catcher Mike LaValliere says he makes a habit of talking to the batter to get his mind off the pitcher. "If there's a batter who is wearing us out, I'll talk to him about his family, the weather, anything but baseball. Most hitters don't like that—and I know they don't like it—especially good hitters like Glenn Davis [of the Astros] and Jack Clark [of the Cardinals]. I try to say something to them every time they get up just to break their concentration. I'll tell them they're not going to see this pitch or that pitch tonight."

Royals third baseman Kevin Seitzer doesn't want to talk to any catcher even if it means hurting his feelings. "The other day Floyd Rayford was catching for the Orioles, and when I came up to bat, he said something to me. But I was so much into the situation and wanted to keep my concentration that I didn't even answer him. So Floyd said, 'Well, I guess I better shut up then.' I think he thought I was angry at him. I wasn't. I just wasn't going to let him disrupt my concentration."

Catchers often try to be helpful, said Mariners hurler Jerry Reed with tongue in cheek. "Catchers have told batters, 'Watch out. He's a little wild today.' They do that just to put another thought in the hitter's mind."

National Leaguers say Gary Carter of the Mets loves to chat—but sometimes he doesn't know when to clam up. When infielder Jerry Royster led off for the Padres in a game against the Mets during the first month of the 1986 season, Carter babbled on and on to him about the off-season. "Meanwhile," Royster recalled, "Dwight Gooden was standing on the mound waiting to throw the first pitch of the game. Finally, the umpire turned to Gary and said, 'Listen, if I could bother you for a moment. Why don't you let Jerry hit and you can continue this the next time he comes up.' "

Rather than carry on a conversation with the hitter, catchers have been known to banter with the home plate umpire—with the same distracting results for the batter. "I don't like it when the catcher carries on a conversation with the ump while the pitcher is in his windup," says Rick Manning. "One time it got so bad that I turned around and said, 'Hey, if you guys want to talk, then wait until after the game and go out to dinner. Just let me hit in peace.' "

Catchers don't yell the typical Little League refrain of "Hey, batter, batter"—that's considered bush. But they aren't afraid to gibe at a hitter every now and then. Recalled White Sox shortstop Ozzie Guillen: "The other day I took three pitches in a row and Terry Kennedy [of the Orioles] said, 'Hey, Ozzie, how do you feel? Are you all right?' I said 'Sure.' And he said, 'How can you take three pitches in a row like that? Don't you know you're supposed to swing at those?' "

Rangers veteran utility man Tom Paciorek claims none of today's catchers can match the late All-Star catcher Thurman Munson of the Yankees when it comes to verbally cutting down the batter. "Thurman was a master. Once I was called on to pinch-hit against the Yankees in the ninth inning when we were a couple of runs down. Thurman looked up and saw me coming to the plate to hit against Goose Gossage and he told me, 'With you up to bat, what are you guys doing? Giving up?' I had to laugh and three pitches later I was back on the bench."

NASTY BAT

Giants slugger Jeffrey Leonard figured out how to shut up talkative catchers who tried to break his concentration at the plate.

He wielded a special bat. In place of his signature on the barrel of the bat were carved the words "FUCK YOU." He took his stance and slowly waved the barrel in front of the catcher's face.

TALKIN' BASEBALL

Not all batters are annoyed by chatty catchers. In fact, many conversations at home plate are initiated by hitters. Here are some examples:

George Frazier, Twins pitcher: "When I was with the Cubs, I once went up to bat against the Mets and told [catcher] Gary Carter, 'Tell your pitcher just to throw three straight down the middle. I'm gonna take three and then go sit down.' He agreed and the first pitch was right down the middle. I hit a line drive up the middle for a base hit. Carter was cussing me all the way up the first-base line."

Mark Grant, Padres pitcher: "I had to bat against Nolan Ryan [of the Astros] and I wasn't looking forward to that. I took the first pitch for a ball and I told [catcher] Alan Ashby, 'Gosh, I didn't even see that one.' When the count went to 1-and-2, I told Alan, 'Hey, don't put a wrinkle on it [call for a curve] because I won't have a chance.' He said, 'Okay.' The next pitch was a fastball right down the shoot and I said, 'I'll see you later.'"

Mets pitcher: "I once convinced [Cardinals catcher] Tony Peña to help me at the plate in the last inning of a blowout. I said, 'Tony, how about telling me what's coming?' Tony agreed and told me, 'Fastball, outside corner,' It was. Then he gave me the location and type of pitch on the next four pitches. I hit the ball hard, but I lined out to short."

Steve Lyons, White Sox: "I grew up in Eugene, Oregon, and I used to watch [Angels catcher] Bob Boone play minor league baseball there. So the first time I ever batted against the Angels, I thought it was neat that Boone was catching. I just had to say something to him so I said, 'Bob, do you know I have a bat of yours?' And he asked me, 'Where did you get it?' I told him, 'I got it when I was 10 years old and you were playing in Eugene.' He gave me this funny look like he was about ready to tell me where I could go. I think I reminded him of how old he was getting."

Steve Lombardozzi, Twins: "During the *Game of the Week* in 1986, I was digging into the box when I farted. The catcher was Jamie Quirk [of the Royals] and he said, 'Thanks for blowing that in my face.' "

NAME THAT TUNE

Some catchers look forward to seeing Mookie Wilson of the Mets come to bat. It's not that he's an easy out. "I have a habit of always humming a tune when I'm at the plate," Wilson explains. "It keeps me relaxed. I hum a different song every time. So catchers always ask me, 'What's the tune for today, Mookie?' "

 ## WHICH CATCHERS ARE MOST ADEPT AT TRICKING UMPIRES INTO CALLING BORDERLINE PITCHES STRIKES?

1. **Bob Boone**
2. **Gary Carter**
3. **Carlton Fisk**

Players in both leagues are in near total agreement that no one "steals" pitches better than Bob Boone of the Angels.

"There will be ten pitches a game out of the strike zone that he'll get called strikes," marvels Royals reserve catcher Jamie Quirk. Adds the Tigers' Dave Bergman, "Bob Boone is incredible. He's a master at bringing balls back into the strike zone."

Since 1972, the light-hitting Boone, who has been on six division winners, has dedicated himself to the finer points of catching. He's the recognized expert of "framing" the pitch on the nearest outside corner of the plate to cleverly get the umpire to make the strike call.

To understand Boone's technique, imagine the strike zone as a painting and a four-inch-wide strip bordering the strike zone as the painting's frame. Pitches thrown within the border (the frame) are caught by Boone, who discreetly brings the ball into the strike zone (the painting) just enough to make the umpire think it's a strike.

"Everybody knows he does it, but he keeps getting away with it," says Steve Lyons of the White Sox. "He's so good that he doesn't move his body. If the ball is four inches outside the strike zone, he'll keep the inside of his glove in the strike zone and just barely catch the ball in the webbing. The umpire looks at the glove and the way it's positioned over the plate and calls it a strike."

This is why players contend Boone steals pitches. But Boone denies being a "thief." Says Boone, "You can't steal strikes at all. I present a picture to the umpire so that he can see that a borderline pitch that is a strike looks like a strike."

Boone catches with "soft hands." He explains: "When I catch a ball, I try to use very fluid, natural movements so that the ball always appears to come back to the center of my body. The idea is to catch the ball with your body in the strike zone. If I do it right and the picture that I'm presenting to the umpire looks good, then the good borderline pitch will look better than if it were caught improperly.

"Many catchers tend to catch borderline pitches improperly by stabbing at them and then trying to move them into the strike zone with sharp quick movements. That only makes the pitches look worse."

Besides Boone, catchers most adept at stealing pitches are Gary Carter of the Mets and Carlton Fisk of the White Sox, according to the *Baseball Confidential* survey. Like Boone, they have their glove ready in position to make it look like the pitch they caught is exactly where it was supposed to be thrown. "Carter can get his pitcher a half-dozen more strikes than he should and that just frosts me," says a Reds player. Adds Steve Lyons, "Fisk is so smooth back there, he can run a clinic on how to get those pitches called strikes."

Ironically for Boone and his pitchers, he might be *too* good at framing pitches. He says his reputation is working against him because umpires are getting tougher on him. "During the last couple of years, the umps haven't been giving me as many borderline calls as before because they know I'm good at it and they think they're going to get tricked. I've had umpires tell me, 'You're not going to get me today. I'm aware of what you do, so I'm going to be a little more critical of you on borderline pitches.' This is upsetting to me because, honestly, I'm not trying to steal a pitch."

WHICH PLAYERS COMPLAIN THE MOST TO HOME PLATE UMPIRES?

1. **Rickey Henderson**
2. **Dwight Evans**
3. **Doug DeCinces**
4. **Gary Carter**
5. **Carlton Fisk**

Since umpires are behind the plate only every fourth day and starters are out there daily, many batters claim they know the strike zone better than the men in blue. And when there's a difference of opinion over a strike call, these players aren't afraid to complain.

"I've been kicked out of every park in the National League," boasts Bill Madlock, who now plays for the Tigers. "I've questioned all the umps." Maybe so. But Madlock is not the biggest complainer— or beggar, as they're known in the bigs. According to the *Baseball Confidential* survey, the worst beggar of all is Rickey Henderson of the Yankees. The consensus is that Henderson never thinks that any pitch he takes is a strike.

"He just works over home plate umpires," said a teammate. "There isn't a game that he doesn't complain at least once. What gets the umps upset is that he looks at them when he's complaining. Rickey makes a big display of it and gestures with his hands. He knows umps hate that."

Ray Miller, former manager of the Twins, says that every time a strike is called on Henderson, "it's a 20-minute ordeal." Miller claimed that during a game in 1986, Rickey whined so much that umpire Tim Welke began calling balls on pitches that should have been strikes to Henderson.

Dwight Evans of the Red Sox "complains about every strike that he doesn't swing at," says Indians hurler Scott Bailes. "He's always telling the ump that the ball is too low or too far inside."

Angels third baseman Doug DeCinces makes sure his feelings are known to the ump whenever he takes a pitch for a strike, admits one of his teammates. "He's always giving the umpire a funny look, a protest, a shake of the head. You can almost set your watch by it."

Batters aren't the only ones complaining at home plate. Catchers do their share of begging too. "Gary Carter [of the Mets] complains more than anybody," declares Phillies pitcher Kevin Gross. Wallace Johnson of the Expos concurs. "Carter will whine on every pitch that's called a ball and he does it so often that the ump will finally call that same pitch a strike. The umps respect Carter, so if he whines about a pitch, then the ump thinks it must be a strike. I've seen it happen many times," Johnson reported.

White Sox veteran catcher Carlton Fisk knows how to work on an umpire, says Bobby Meacham of the Yankees. "When he complains, he makes the ump aware that his pitcher needs a certain pitch to be effective, and if it's close, he wants to get that pitch." Fisk wants the ump to call strikes on every pitch—even when it's four inches off the plate, contends Gary Roenicke of the Braves. "When I was in the American League, I wanted to get equal time when Fisk started begging for strikes." Blue Jays third baseman Kelly Gruber says that whenever he took a pitch that just missed the corner, he'd hear Fisk trying to pressure the umpire into calling the next similar pitch a strike. "It would be a foot outside and Fisk would say, 'That's close, let's go, make that call. That's too close for this guy to take.' "

Says Angels pitcher DeWayne Buice, "There's something about catchers. They think that if they protect the umpire from getting hit by a ball, they deserve some extra calls in their favor."

WHAT DO UMPIRES SAY TO BATTERS WHO COMPLAIN OVER A CALLED THIRD STRIKE?

When ringing up a batter, the ump often says a lot more than "Strike three, you're out!" Here's a sampling:

Kirby Puckett, Twins: "Ken Kaiser is something else. I swung at a ball that bounced in front of the plate, then I swung at one that was much too high, and I took the next pitch for strike three. I argued over the pitch and Kaiser snapped, 'You swing at a fucking ball in the dirt, you swing at a fucking ball over your head, and then you take one right down the middle. Go fucking sit down!' "

Bill Madlock, Tigers—When Madlock was in the National League, he once asked plate umpire Bruce Froemming a typical question on a questionable third strike. "I asked him, 'Where was that ball?' And Bruce said, 'What is this, a fucking quiz or something? Just get the fuck outta here!' "

Al Newman, Twins—Teammates still talk about the time their third-year reserve infielder argued over a third strike with Durwood Merrill. The arbiter told Newman, "Go sit down. You don't have enough dirt in your spikes to talk to me like that!"

Floyd Rayford, Orioles—Rayford says he knows better than to tangle with Ken Kaiser. According to Rayford, the umpire finished airing him out during a game by snarling, "Shit, you're lucky to be in the majors. You're on a wing and a prayer to be here anyway."

George Bamberger, Brewers manager—Durwood Merrill once blasted Bamberger with a double-barrel putdown. After Bambi stuck up for his player, who was protesting a third strike, Merrill called the manager out of the dugout and said, "You're starting to act more and more like Earl Weaver every day." Merrill started walking back to his position and then turned around and shouted, "Not only that, but you're starting to look like Earl too!"

Steve Lyons, White Sox—Lyons says that when he was a rookie, he didn't know whether to laugh or cry after he questioned Jerry Neudecker over a third strike. "I said, 'Man, that pitch was high.' And he said, 'You don't say that to me. You *ask* me if that pitch was high.' So I said, 'All right, was the pitch high?' And he replied, 'Yeah, it was. But I still called it a strike and that means you're out.' I ended up laughing all the way back to the dugout."

THE RIGHT WAY AND WRONG WAY TO COMPLAIN

If batters are upset over a called strike, they can swear, bitch, or groan—just as long as they do it quietly and, most importantly, don't look at the umpire.

"The key is not to turn around at the umpire because the minute you make eye contact, he feels you're showing him up in front of everyone," says Rick Manning of the Brewers. "Then he gets pissed off and it can do you no good."

Von Hayes of the Phillies learned that lesson in 1987. "Von took a 2-and-0 pitch and [home plate umpire] Lee Weyer called it a strike," recounted Phillies coach Claude Osteen. "Von took his bat and drew a line lengthwise in the batter's box about four inches from the plate. And in a sarcastic voice, he told Weyer, 'That was a perfect pitch, Lee. It went right across here.' Twelve thousand fans saw Von show up the umpire. What did it get him? Lee racked him up on the next two pitches."

Bob Dernier of the Cubs says he seldom turns around when questioning a call. "Sometimes [umpire] Eric Gregg will call a high fastball a strike and without looking at him I'll tell him, 'I don't want those high fastball calls. This is a low-ball league and you're destroying the strike zone. I'd rather you called those low outside pitches strikes because at least they're low.' You can get away with talk like that as long as you're staring straight ahead."

More than anything, according to the players, umpires hate it when a batter tries to start for first base on a 3-and-1 pitch that is called a strike. "After that happens, if the next pitch is within a foot of the plate, you can bet the ump is going to call it a strike," said a Pirate.

If a batter is called out on strikes on a pitch that he knows was a ball, he can make a statement without saying a word, according to

Mike Easler of the Yankees. "You can walk away and throw your bat and helmet toward the dugout without looking at the ump. He can't be sure whether you're mad at him or yourself. Or you can drop your bat and helmet very nicely at home plate. I try to be cool about it."

Some players try to get on the umpire's good side by talking to him, always smiling or joking around at the plate, thinking that maybe they will get a break. But that won't work, says Kent Tekulve of the Phillies. "I've found over the years that the umps are no dummies. They know what the batters are up to. Usually, an ump will do just the opposite. I like to see a batter talk to the ump because I feel then I have the advantage. The ump knows that everyone has seen this guy try to be his buddy and so the ump is going to bend over backward not to give him any breaks."

▲

SWEET NOTHINGS

Tom Paciorek of the Rangers says he loves the way teammate Pete Incaviglia sweet-talks umpires whenever he questions one of their calls at the plate. "He uses cute little sayings like 'I'm gonna murder you' or 'I'm gonna pinch your head off.' "

▲

VETERANS DAY AT HOME PLATE

The better veteran hitters generally enjoy a slight advantage on balls and strikes over the younger players.

"A rookie is not going to get the same call that a Mike Schmidt gets," says Mets coach Bill Robinson. "On borderline pitches, the call will go to a Mike Schmidt."

Today there are several "Don't-call-a-strike-on-me" players, who, because of their reputation for having a sharp batting eye, get more than their fair share of close pitches called balls. Among the players who benefit from this largess are such hitters as Wade Boggs, Don Mattingly, George Brett, and Tony Gwynn.

"Umpires don't want to cause a ruckus, so if it's a borderline pitch thrown by a young pitcher who hasn't been around very long, the umps are more apt to give the pitch to the veteran hitter," says Butch Wynegar of the Angels.

Adds a teammate, "Boggs's batting eye is so good that umpires rarely call strikes against him. In the National League, Pete Rose didn't have those borderline strikes called on him because his reputation as a hitter had such an influence on the umpires."

This special veterans' influence works behind the plate as well. Catchers like Carlton Fisk and Bob Boone have been in the league for so long that they know all the umpires and have gained their respect. As a result, says Mike Boddicker of the Orioles, "They're always telling the umpire that those balls he's calling are really strikes and soon the ump begins to believe them. Meanwhile, they're just moving their glove further and further out until all of a sudden the plate is four inches wider.

"It can work for the pitchers too. If there's a veteran on the mound who's known to throw strikes and is consistently around the strike zone year after year, he's going to get those borderline strikes."

There's not much young batters can do about it. "As a rookie coming into the league, I learned it doesn't do any good for me to argue," said Paul Runge of the Braves. "It just compounds the problem. I don't need the added burden of arguing with the ump. You have to prove yourself in this league."

Whenever they question a strike, some respected veterans can get away with saying much more to an umpire than most players can, says Phillies coach Claude Osteen. "For example, the other night Mike Schmidt questioned a call and he said more than he should. You might see that once every five years with him. The umps know he's almost always good about accepting their calls, so they'll bend a little and he'll get a lot of borderline pitches called in his favor."

WHAT DO HOME PLATE UMPIRES DO TO TICK PLAYERS OFF?

1. **Call balls and strikes inconsistently**
2. **Show quick tempers when players question their calls**
3. **Hold grudges against certain players**
4. **Call the pitch before it reaches the strike zone**
5. **Expand the strike zone to speed up the game**

Far and away the biggest complaint batters have about home plate umpires is their lack of consistency in calling balls and strikes.

"Nothing ticks me off more than to have an inconsistent umpire behind the plate," says four-time batting champion Bill Madlock. "If an ump calls an obvious ball a strike, then the batter is going to swing at the next ball no matter where it's thrown. I try not to do that, but it happens."

Although many umps were accused of inconsistency calls in the *Baseball Confidential* survey, the names most frequently mentioned by players were Fred Brocklander and Jim Quick of the National League and the junior circuit's Greg Kosc, Vic Voltaggio, and Dale Ford. "There's no rhyme or reason to some umps' calls," said a veteran AL catcher. "You don't know where you stand when you go behind the plate." Adds an NL pitcher, "Brocklander misses some calls when he goes into a time warp." George Frazier of the Twins has a theory on which umps miss the most calls: "They're probably the single umps who keep looking up in the stands at the beef."

One outfielder listed Dale Ford among the worst umpires in baseball because of his alleged inconsistency. "If you yell at him, then he'll stick it up your butt the whole game," said the player.

Several National Leaguers cited Frank Pulli as an arbiter who seeks revenge against players who question him. "During spring training, Pulli called a terrible pitch a strike against a rookie," recalls

Phillies catcher Darren Daulton. "The rookie questioned the call and Frank jumped all over him. So I thought I'd help the kid and set up a foot outside on the next two pitches. Frank rang him up for no reason at all. The guy started arguing again and I told him, 'Hey, it's not going to do you any good.' "

Among the biggest complaints among batters is the confrontational attitude taken by many umpires. "The young ones seem to think that the best way to gain respect right away is to be a hard-ass," says Graig Nettles of the Braves. "They could get that respect simply by calling a good, consistent game. The best compliment you can give an umpire is that you don't remember who called the game. But some of the younger ones want to make a name for themselves and go out of their way to be controversial."

Adds veteran catcher Butch Wynegar of the Angels, "If you ask them a very simple question, right away they're on your back and flying off the handle like you just cussed out their mother. The most confrontational is John Shulock. If you ask him a question about a pitch, he gets rednecked at you very quickly. He's a good umpire and everything but his personality gets in the way." Athletics pitching star Dave Stewart concurs. "Shulock is not personable, does not want to make any friends, does not want to crack jokes, does not want to talk. He's always trying to establish the fact that he's in control of the game. That means sometimes he's got the red ass.

"I've had my differences with Tim McClelland but they've been resolved. He's a personable guy but sometimes he wants to establish that he's in control a little bit too much instead of relaxing and being a good umpire."

Players in the survey griped that too many umpires will hold a grudge against a player for years. For example, says Bill Almon of the Mets, "some umps have short fuses and if you question them just once, they'll remember that and stick it to you five years down the road."

Tony Gwynn says he won't argue over any pitches with ump Charlie Williams because "I don't like him—it's that simple. He screwed me in Triple A and I think he remembers screwing me. I hit a ground ball and beat the play to first but Charlie called me out. I said, 'Charlie, I beat that ball.' And he said, 'If you say one more word, I'm going to wring your ass out of here.' I said, 'All right. I'll remember that.' And I have. I haven't forgotten."

Umpire Bill Williams won't get a beef from Bob Dernier of the Cubs. Explains Dernier. "When I was a rookie [in 1980], I argued a strike-three call once with Williams. As I was walking back toward the dugout, he said, 'Hey, kid, come here.' I turned around and saw him walking toward me pretty fast and he said, 'Don't ever talk to me again.' That pretty much convinced me. Although I like to argue with umpires, I never argue with him."

Umpires who anticipate the pitch before it crosses the plate also rile players. Recalled a San Diego player, "I saw that happen in 1987 in a game in Atlanta. Dion James [of the Braves] was at the plate and while the pitch was on the way, the ump, Harry Wendelstedt, was already ringing him up—and the ball never reached the catcher because James hit it foul."

A member of the Giants said he'll never forget the game in 1984 when Dave Pallone *forgot* to make the call on a pitch and it cost the team the game. "It was the bottom of the 12th inning of a tie game in St. Louis and Glenn Brummer of the Cards was the runner on third base. There were two outs and a 3-and-2 count on the batter. On the pitch, Brummer broke for the plate and Pallone moved out from behind home plate to the side to make the call. He called Brummer safe—but he never called the pitch! The call lost the game for the Giants. Some of the Cards admitted that the pitch was a strike. Pallone has been involved in other situations where he has anticipated the play and made the call before it even had been completed."

Players get bugged by home plate umpires who hurry the game along. "I hate it when they try to speed up the game because they have a plane to catch," says Gary Gaetti of the Twins. "All of a sudden the strike zone gets bigger than normal." Kirk Gibson of the Tigers said he learned all about expanding strike zones when he was a rookie. "During one game that was dragging on and on, the ump told me he had a plane to catch and that I'd better be swinging—and not only at things that were close. He wasn't kidding because I was out of there real quick.

"Sometimes I can tell when the ump is hurrying things along. If a called strike is questionable, I might ask the umpire, 'Do you have a plane to catch tonight?' And he'll look at his watch and say, 'Yeah, now shut up and get back in the box. It's getting late.' "

▲ HOT PLATE

Once it got so hot behind the plate that an umpire actually urged a pitcher to throw strikes.

"[Umpire] Durwood Merrill can make me laugh," says Royals pitcher Mark Gubicza. "I was pitching on a hot day and Merrill, who was behind the plate, kept telling me, 'Come on, Gubie, let's throw strikes. I want to get out of here. It's too hot.' I said, 'Fine, just call me a few strikes.' And he said, 'Okay, I'll call you a few. We both want to get out of here and have a beer, don't we?' "

WHO ARE THE BEST HOME PLATE UMPIRES?

National League:
1. **Bruce Froemming**
2. **Dutch Rennert**
3. **Doug Harvey**

American League:
1. **Steve Palermo**
2. **Ken Kaiser**
3. **Rich Garcia**

According to the *Baseball Confidential* survey, these are the umpires players most want to see behind the plate. Sure, they all miss some calls now and then and they do have their detractors. But they have gained the respect of the players for being fair—and, in some cases, fun.

"Bruce Froemming is respected as a good umpire and is in total control of the game," says Phillies coach Claude Osteen. "He won't put up with anything or let the game get out of hand. You don't question too many of his balls and strikes because he's good." Tony Gwynn says he never questions Froemming out of respect because "when he makes a call, that's it—he knows what he's doing."

So does veteran umpire Dutch Rennert, says Wallace Johnson of the Expos. "When he calls something a strike, you know it's a strike. He has a very distinctive call and he has a lot of confidence behind the plate."

Echoing the views of many National Leaguers, Gwynn said, "Doug Harvey feels very sure of himself behind the plate and he's not afraid to let you speak your mind if you disagree. But you seldom need to disagree with him."

Butch Wynegar is one of many American League players who rate Steve Palermo and Ken Kaiser as their favorites. "I think Palermo is the best in the league because he works hard and is very consistent behind the plate. Kaiser is right up there with him. Very rarely would I question a ball or strike called by either one. I can never remember getting angry at them for anything they did." Says Sammy Stewart of the Indians, "Kaiser gives you a fair shake and so does Palermo. I like Palermo a lot because he's heads-up and very enthusiastic. He gets into the game. He's interesting to talk to and he makes the game fun." Kevin Seitzer of the Royals rates Palermo tops because "he's good and he knows he's good. Very seldom do you question one of his calls. If you do, he'll tell you right where he thought it was. And if he thinks he missed one, he'll tell you. I respect an umpire who admits his mistakes."

Rich Garcia is considered among the best because of his consistency, says Dan Plesac of the Brewers. "He's made some tough calls, but I haven't seen one yet that I thought was bad." Adds a Yankee, "At least when I go up to bat, I don't have to worry about a bad call with Garcia."

Other plate arbiters have their admirers too. For example, Seitzer says he appreciates the honesty of ump John Hirshbeck. "The other night he called a strike on me that was low and out of the strike zone. The next time I came up he told me, I missed that one. I said, 'I know. That's why I didn't say anything to you. I figured you knew.'"

Jerry Royster, who spent 14 years in the National League before going to the White Sox, names Jim Quick as his favorite umpire. The NL arbiter hails from Marysville, California, right outside of Sacramento, where Royster was born and raised. "He's a good umpire plus he's one of my homies, so I figure he's given me the benefit of the doubt on close pitches," said Royster. "Whenever he made a call which I thought was questionable, he would ask me my opinion the following time up when nobody was around. He has phoned me after the game and asked me what I thought."

Pirates catcher Mike LaValliere says the best times behind the plate are with umpire Bob Davidson. "Bob and I talk about everything from what's on the front page to who I think will win the football game. It just makes the job a little bit easier for him and me. Some umps are so darn uptight that it inhibits them. If they would relax a little bit, they'd probably be better umpires."

BIGGEST SHOWBOAT UMPIRES

1. Durwood Merrill, AL
2. Eric Gregg, NL
3. Dutch Rennert, NL
4. Frank Pulli NL
5. Ken Kaiser, AL

 ## WHICH UMPIRES HAVE THE QUICKEST THUMBS?

American League:	*National League:*
1. **Ken Kaiser**	1. **Paul Runge**
2. **Steve Palermo**	2. **Joe West**
3. **Joe Brinkman**	3. **Dave Pallone**

To hear the players tell it, umpires today have little patience for debating a call. The men in blue are simply putting up with less guff—and that irks players.

"Some of the younger American League umps won't let you talk with them," says the Braves' Gary Roenicke, a former AL player. "If you can't talk to umpires, that's pretty bad. They'll provoke you until you're pretty hot and then you say something and boom you're out of the game. You say one word and they rip the mask off, shout back, and run you."

A National League All-Star complained that umpires are hurting the game by needlessly tossing players out for speaking their mind. "If I'm a fan paying to see a star play and the ump kicks him out of the game, I'm going to demand my money back. What gives the ump the right to deprive me of seeing the star I paid money to watch? I didn't come to see the umpire. Players should be able to complain without fear of getting run. When the ump fucks up, shouldn't he get kicked out too?"

For umpires, ejections are part of the job. It's just that some do it more quickly than others. Even though he's considered among the best umps, Ken Kaiser has the quickest thumb in the American League today, according to the *Baseball Confidential* survey. "You can't say two words to Kaiser before he's all over you," says a member of the Red Sox. "He gets indignant if you challenge him about anything—or even if you ask him a question." Adds Gary Redus of the White Sox, "I don't say too much to him because he's pretty quick with the thumb. The word is to stay away from him."

The second-shortest fuse in the AL belongs to Steve Palermo, say the players. "He jumps right down your shorts the moment you open your mouth," claims a Royal. Adds Lenn Sakata of the Yankees, "Palermo is so tempermental. He doesn't want to hear arguments from anybody. When I was with Baltimore, Palermo ejected Eddie Murray for laughing. I had tried to steal second and Palermo called me out so I laid on the ground. Murray started laughing at me from the dugout. Palermo thought Eddie was laughing at him and gave him the thumb. After the game, Eddie tried to talk to him and even called the umpire's room, but Palermo wouldn't talk to him."

Joe Brinkman comes in third on the quick heave-ho list. "He'll get pissed off if you give him a dirty look," said an Oriole. "He'll cuss you out and if you talk back, you're history." Bobby Meacham of the Yankees didn't even get a chance to talk back before getting run by Brinkman. "I had a smirk on my face over a bad call he made in the previous inning and Brinkman began screaming at me and saying, 'Who are you laughing at?' I tried to ignore him, but by now he was right in my face, so I said, 'You,' and he threw me out of the game."

Tom Brunansky of the Twins says Brinkman ejected him for swearing at himself. "In 1985, I argued with him over a strike and on the next pitch, I hit a weak tap back to the pitcher. As I turned toward the third-base dugout, I ran between the mound and home plate, swearing at myself for being stupid to swing at such a bad pitch. Brinkman thought I was swearing at him, and before I even got to the dugout, he threw me out of the game."

Over in the senior circuit, Paul Runge runs players the quickest, according to the survey. "He throws out a lot of young players," says Tim Flannery of the Padres. "He likes to set his ground very early with you and then the more years you play, the better he is with you. He ejected me in my first full year in the league in 1980. I got my face so close to him that my hat hit the rim of his hat and knocked it into his eyes. Two seconds later I was gone." Several Phillies complained that early in 1987, Runge dispatched their teammate, catcher Lance Parrish, for nothing more than holding the ball an extra second on a ball-four call and asking, "Was that low?"

Although players say that Joe West seems to be mellowing, he still has one of the league's quickest thumbs. "He's not the type that likes conversation," says a player. "His way of telling you to shut up is to run you." West holds the dubious honor of being the first umpire to ever eject two TV cameramen from a game. It happened in 1984 when the cameramen were in the Mets dugout showing the players an instant replay of a contested play that West had called. After viewing the replay, the Mets let West know he had blown the call. West retaliated by kicking the cameramen out of the dugout.

"To me," says a Met, "there's a tie between West and Dave Pallone for the quickest thumb. At least West has a reason for what he does. Pallone has no reason for his actions and will throw somebody out for nothing—and at the spur of the moment." After being run by Pallone in 1987, Dave Concepcion of the Reds complained to the press that Pallone has a vendetta against him. "They've had a running feud for years," says a teammate. "Pallone is out to get him. You can't have that in baseball."

WHICH BATTERS ARE BEST AT PSYCHING OUT PITCHERS?

1. **Dave Winfield**
2. **Don Baylor**
3. **Jack Clark**
4. **Dave Parker**

Hitters most adept at unnerving pitchers don't necessarily lead the league in homers or batting average. Instead, they're the hitters who, through reputation and swagger, have a presence that instills real fear in the hurler.

Named most often in the *Baseball Confidential* survey as the batsman best at psyching out pitchers is Yankees superstar Dave Winfield. At 6 feet, 6 inches, 220 pounds, Winfield "stands like a giant up there," said an Indians hurler. "It's not that I fear him hitting a homer off me. I fear him killing me with one of those shots of his. He hits the ball so damn hard and I'm only 60 feet, 6 inches away."

Winfield's teammate, Wayne Tolleson, says he enjoys the way Winfield coolly plays mind games with pitchers. "He's so good at it, the way he digs in, glares at the pitcher, and keeps his bat moving all the time." Adds Jesse Barfield of the Blue Jays, "Winfield stares right through a pitcher. Sometimes pitchers don't want to admit it, but that can intimidate them."

Red Sox designated hitter Don Baylor goes out of his way to psych out pitchers. "His whole demeanor is intimidating," says Royals hurler Bud Black. "He stands over the plate like he owns it and doesn't smile. He's old-school baseball and he's tough." Baylor admits trying to unnerve the pitcher during every at-bat. "That's part of the game," he says. "If a pitcher throws at me, I'll get a little closer to the plate the next time and say, 'I dare you to try that again.' That's probably why I've been hit so many times—yet I've never missed a game from being hit by a pitch."

Like Baylor, Cardinals slugger Jack Clark presents such an imposing figure at the plate that some pitchers get spooked. Says

Kevin McReynolds of the Mets, "Pitchers know he's going to get his licks in and if they make a mistake they'll have to pay for it." Mets pitching coach Mel Stottlemyre says Clark's psych job begins when he digs at the plate and stares at the pitcher. "Just the way he presents himself makes you not want to throw the ball anywhere where he can swing at it."

Reflecting the sentiments of many fellow hurlers, Bob Walk of the Pirates says Dave Parker has been messing up the minds of pitchers for more than a decade. "He's so big and he swings that bat around as if it weighs only 10 ounces. He pounds that baby on the plate. And pitchers think, 'God, I don't want to even throw this pitch.' You look at him and he's got so much confidence that he's going to get a hit. And he doesn't smile."

It's a fact of baseball life that certain hitters will psych out pitchers, says veteran reliever Kent Tekulve of the Phillies. "With some batters it doesn't matter what the first pitch is or where it's at, they're going to swing at it with all their might, trying to convince the pitcher that they're just sitting all over the fastball. Usually, these batters are also good breaking-ball hitters trying to scare the pitcher from throwing the fastball so they can get the breaking ball instead.

"Then there are batters like Bill Buckner [of the Red Sox] who's very good at setting up pitchers. When someone throws inside, Buckner looks like he's going to charge the mound, hoping the ump will warn the pitcher that the next such pitch will get him ejected. The truth is Buckner never wants to hit the inside pitch. He wants the outside pitch. If Buckner gets the ump to give the warning, then he can sit on the outside pitch for the rest of the day. That way, he ends up with two more hits than he would have normally gotten if the pitcher could have pitched him hard inside."

AND THE WINNER FOR BEST ACTOR IS . . .

Cubs third-base coach John Vukovich began calling All-Star second baseman Ryne Sandberg "Gregory Peck" for his performance in snowing home plate umpire Dick Stello during a game in 1987.

While batting against the Braves' David Palmer with runners on first and second and no outs, Sandberg ducked away from an inside fastball that appeared to graze the bat handle. But Sandberg let out a yelp and immediately grabbed his left wrist. He looked like he had been hit by the pitch and appeared to be in a great deal of pain. He even called out the trainer as Vukovich and a few teammates crowded around him.

After looking at the wincing Sandberg, a sympathetic Stello ruled Ryno had been hit by the pitch. Braves manager Chuck Tanner raced out of the dugout to protest, claiming the ball had hit the bat and not Sandberg's wrist. But Stello bellowed, "Get back. The kid almost broke his hand."

Just before heading down to first base, Sandberg turned to Vukovich, gave him a wink and a grin, and whispered, "I sure deked him, didn't I?"

THINGS BATTERS DO TO IRK PITCHERS

Rick Mahler, Braves: "It kind of bugs me when Keith Hernandez [of the Mets] is the third hitter in the inning and he's in the on-deck circle just staring at me."

Dave Smith, Astros: "It's annoying when Pedro Guerrero [of the Dodgers] keeps stepping out of the box all the time. And if you walk him, he tosses the bat in a way that says, 'You're afraid to pitch to me' when you're not."

Bud Black, Royals: "George Bell [of the Blue Jays] kept digging and digging and digging in the batter's box and finally called time out because he said he needed more time to dig. He wanted to make it a point that he wanted to dig in on me and I didn't appreciate that."

Paul Assenmacher, Braves: "Some batters step out of the batter's box in a crucial situation to add tension to the moment and to make sure that they are the center of attention."

Rangers pitcher: "Mark McGwire [of the A's] never takes his hands off his bat from the time he gets to the on-deck circle until he's through at the plate. His two hands are on there the whole time as if he's telling the pitcher that he means business."

DOCTORED BATS

On September 2, 1987, Billy Hatcher, one of the Astros' best hitters, broke his bat on an infield single. But this was no ordinary bat. The split lumber revealed that the barrel contained three to four inches of cork. Umpire crew chief John McSherry disallowed Hatcher's single and ejected him from the game. Despite Hatcher's contention that he unwittingly grabbed the corked bat—which he claimed was owned by a teammate as a joke—Hatcher was suspended by the league for ten days.

Hatcher was the first and only batter of the 1987 season to be caught, but players in the *Baseball Confidential* survey admit that occasionally hitters wield loaded bats. Although corked bats have been around for years, the 1987 season produced more accusations of cheating than ever before.

Time and again, the Mets' Howard Johnson, whose previous career high in homers was 13 but who belted 36 in 1987, was accused of swinging an illegal bat. So were Pedro Guerrero of the Dodgers and Candy Maldonado of the Giants. But when their bats were confiscated and X-rayed, the examinations revealed the bats were legit.

"There are players right now using loaded bats," said a veteran. "They don't use them every game, but every now and then. Pitchers scuff the ball, so why can't hitters doctor the bat?"

A common way to cork a bat is to drill a hole 12 to 14 inches down into the barrel without splitting the wood and then pack the hole tight with ground-up cork, leaving a two-inch void at the top. The hole is then closed with a carefully shaped plug of plastic wood that is sanded over the top of the bat. With a corked center, the mass of a 36-ounce bat takes on the whiplash quickness of a 34-ouncer. Players believe a corked bat can add up to 50 feet to a hit.

"At one time, when I was in the Venezuelan League, there were several active major leaguers—some of whom are still playing—who bought cases of doctored bats from a guy who makes them there," claims Ray Miller, former manager of the Twins and now a Pirates coach.

"I've talked to guys who have corked their bats," says Butch

Wynegar. "One player said he was embarrassed because once when he hit the ball off the handle, the ball bounced off the scoreboard in right field." He said the owners of loaded bats usually use them only in a clutch situation.

"There have been times when the manager has ordered me to pick up the bat of an opposing batter after he's hit the ball and check it. But those batboys come out and pick up the bat before I've had time to check it. That sure makes me suspicious.

"The one fear I have is that the first time I use a corked bat, the bat is going to break and they're going to catch me. Then I'll want to crawl into a hole."

THE
DUGOUT

LOOSENING UP IN THE DUGOUT

The dugout atmosphere may hang heavy with intensity and resolve during a game, but there's often a dose of comic relief going on as well.

Most teams have a resident funnyman like Mets' reliever Roger McDowell, who can lighten the mood of a dugout faster than a 6-4-3 double play. Offering a silent tribute to pitchers accused of doctoring the ball, McDowell sauntered around the dugout in a 1987 game with a carpenter's belt strapped to his waist. The belt contained everything a cheating hurler could want—lubricant, sandpaper, a file, and a chisel. A week later, McDowell glued wine corks on the outside of a practice bat and presented it to his teammate Howard Johnson, who had been accused by the Cardinals of wielding a corked bat.

Earlier in the year in Los Angeles, McDowell livened up the Mets dugout by wearing his uniform upside down. He put his legs in the sleeves of his jersey and pulled his pants down over his head, thrusting his arms through the pant legs. Then he put shoes on his hands. "It was the funniest thing I ever saw in a dugout," said Mets coach Bill Robinson. "I keep wondering where he comes up with these things."

McDowell admits he was a little hesitant to do the stunt. "But with the courage and inspiration of my teammates, I went ahead and did it."

At least Roger's humor isn't gross. The same can't be said for that of Twin Bert Blyleven. "I've seen him put his boogers on people's hats," said former teammate Ken Schrom of the Indians. "He'll do anything for a laugh." That includes picking his nose and eating the boogers right in front of a live TV camera, claims Tom Brunansky of the Twins. Adds teammate Steve Lombardozzi, "When Blyleven picks his nose and eats the boogers, it makes me want to throw up. It's the most disgusting thing I've ever seen in the dugout."

When things get dull in the dugout, Oil Can Boyd of the Red Sox has been known to do his favorite impersonation. "He does a great Stevie Wonder," says teammate Marty Barrett. "Oil Can puts on some sunglasses, gets that smile, and starts singing and waving his head just like Stevie."

Juan Beniquez of the Blue Jays likes to show off a rare talent—throwing his voice. "He'll stand right behind you and shout your name in a voice that sounds like it's far off and coming from the stands," says teammate Mark Eichhorn. "I don't know how he does it but he's great at it. One day in Toronto, [pitcher] Don Gordon was standing on the steps of the dugout and he didn't know Juan was just two feet away. Juan kept shouting for him and Gordy kept looking up in the stands, searching for the person who was calling his name. He had no idea that it was Juan."

During games, some Royals try to inspire and loosen the team up by using "rally caps." When pitcher Joe Beckwith was with the Royals in 1985, he convinced his teammates that wearing their caps inside out in the dugout would bring good luck during a Kansas City rally. But now hurlers Mark Gubicza and Bret Saberhagen have a new version. "We created the land shark look where we have the bill of our caps sticking up in the air to make it look like we're sharks coming in for the kill," Gubicza explains. "Just before the All-Star break, it worked great. We won three games in a row with it. Usually, we use the rally cap in the early part of the game. Then, if we're ahead in the seventh or eighth inning, we become the land sharks and go in for the killing."

The dugout is an excellent venue for pulling off a prank in the middle of a game. Explains rookie Ellis Burks of the Red Sox, "When I got my first hit in the majors, they called time and got the ball from the umpire and threw it in the dugout for me. When I came back in, they said, 'Here's your ball.' Then they dropped it in some spit and chew on the dugout floor. I picked up the ball and tried to dry it off and then another teammate spit on it. I was mad and said, 'Hey, man, c'mon. That's my ball.' Then they all started to laugh. That wasn't my ball. The real one was safe and sitting on the bench."

You don't have to be a rookie to get nailed by a practical joke, says veteran Blue Jay Jesse Barfield. "[Toronto pitcher] José Nuñez taped some toilet paper to my pants in the dugout without me knowing it," said Barfield. "I walked out to the on-deck circle and everyone could see toilet paper hanging from my pants and thinking, 'Jesse didn't wipe his butt.' Fortunately for me, the guys warned me before I got up to the plate. That would have been real terrible because the game was on national television."

A Phillies player recalls the dirty trick that was pulled on teammate Steve Jeltz during a 1986 game. "He had a pretty nice Indiana Jones hat that he kept in the dugout," said the player. "Somebody swiped it during the game without Steve knowing it and took a dump in it. Then the hat was put back. When Steve picked up his hat and discovered what happened, he wasn't a very happy camper."

White Sox catcher Marc Hill shoots a mean can of shaving cream in the dugout, says former teammate Bill Dawley of the Cardinals. "Marc was always putting shaving cream on the top of teammates' hats without them knowing it. They'd walk out onto the field and look like an ass. He didn't care who he got—the manager, coaches, or players."

Even though no smoking is allowed in the dugout, players violate the ban, a practice that led to one of the wackiest sights Mark Grant of the Padres ever witnessed in the dugout. "When I was with the Giants, I saw Duane Kuiper sitting on top of the back of the bench while [coach] Herm Starrette was sitting below him. Kuiper was smoking a cigarette and flicking the ashes on top of Herm's cap. All of a sudden, the cap caught fire and Herm threw it off and we burst out laughing."

▲

HAL OF A HIT

In a fit of rage during a 1987 game, Astros manager Hal Lanier grabbed a bat out of the rack and whaled away at the dugout railing. Pitcher Danny Darwin, realizing that the bat was his, shouted, "Hey, you're using my bat!" Whereupon a still-fuming Lanier snarled, "So what? This is the first thing it's hit all year."

▲

BIG LEAGUE TEMPER TANTRUMS

Most major league hotheads wait until they reach the dugout before flying into a rage over their failure to get a key hit or pitch out of a jam. Here, in the relative privacy of the dugout, the quick-tempered wreak havoc in what some teams call "snaps."

For some unexplained reason, the Royals are loaded with more snappers than any other team in baseball. Their leader, as he is on the field, is George Brett, who awes the club with his tempetuous outbursts. "He's the best," says teammate Jamie Quirk. "One day at Royals Stadium, George made an out and charged into the tunnel where you could hear him beating a trash can with his bat. Then there was silence. I didn't know what the heck was going on so I went to investigate. There was George inside the trash can and all you could see was his head sticking out. Finally, he climbed out and played the next inning with trash all over him."

Even though that snap impressed his teammates, Brett contends it wasn't his worst temper tantrum. "My greatest snap happened in Baltimore in 1986. I had just struck out for the third time in two days and I had to find a release, so I went into the dugout runway and threw my bat. Then I saw a gallon paint can. First, I kicked it and then I threw it up against the wall and it just exploded and paint went all over the place. I picked up the can and saw there was still paint in it. I was going to pour it over my head but I chickened out at the last minute. I always wonder what would have happened if I had poured it over my head and then gone out and played. Right now I wish I had done it. If there's a paint can in our locker room, I just might do it tonight if I go 0-for-5." (Brett went 1-for-4 that night.)

Here are more snappers from the bigs:

Danny Jackson, Royals: He's nicknamed "Captain Snap" or "Jason" (after the character in the *Friday the 13th* movies) by his teammates. "It's frightening to watch a guy get as mad as he does," says teammate Bud Black. "Most of the time you don't dare look at him when he's having a snap." Jackson's best snap of 1987 came after he was shelled early in a game. Recalls teammate Bret Saberhagen, "DJ was so upset he hadn't done well that he ripped everything out of his locker—hats, shoes, gloves, clothes—and threw them in the middle of the clubhouse floor. Then he said, 'I don't want any of this stuff anymore. You can throw it away. Do anything you want with it. I'm getting everything new in here. I'm changing my number. This is the last day I wear 25. I'm wearing 15.' Three days later, he had number 15."

Bret Saberhagen, Royals: "Saberhagen came out of a game

and was steaming mad in the dugout," said Bud Black. "Then he went straight into the shower with his uniform and cleats still on."

Kevin Seitzer, Royals: "My snaps range from 5 to 30 seconds. Then I'm okay. It's just a release I've got to have. The other day, I went back to the dugout and ripped my batting gloves off my hands—just completely shredded them. I had to get new batting gloves for my next at-bat but at least I felt a little bit better."

Kirk Gibson, Tigers—He vents his anger in the dugout the old-fashioned way—he hits things. "When Kirk gets mad, you just get out of his way," says former teammate Howard Johnson of the Mets. "He comes into the dugout and jumps up and down, wants to break everything, yells 'goddamn it!' as loud as he can, and slams his bat."

Bill Doran, Astros—He takes his bat to the dugout tunnel where no one can see him and wears his bat out on his helmet and the walls, says former teammate Frank DiPino of the Cubs. "I always got on him about that. He'd tell me every day, 'You know, I've turned over a new leaf.' And I'd say, 'Let me see your next at-bat.' If he made an out, he'd go back into the tunnel and do it all over again."

Geno Petralli, Rangers—He took on the whole bat rack after striking out, recalls teammate Pete O'Brien. "Geno took his bat and hit every bat in the rack about 20 times in succession. He flat out beat them." No one would have minded except that over the next few days, the Rangers experienced an extraordinary number of broken bats at the plate. "We figure that Geno weakened some of those bats when he hit them," said O'Brien.

Ozzie Guillen, White Sox—Ozzie, who claims he's the only hothead on his team, takes his frustrations out on his helmet. "One time last year I got my helmet and got my bat and hit the helmet about a hundred times and broke it into hundreds of pieces."

Von Hayes, Phillies—He specializes in flinging helmets and destroying water coolers. "During a game against the Mets in 1987, Von stranded five players. So he went into the dugout and started kicking the water cooler and hitting it with his bat until it was annihilated," recalls Philadelphia beat writer Bill Brown. "He broke the mechanism that helped cool the water. A week later, I was coming down the tunnel from the clubhouse and there was Von poking around the guts of the water cooler with the handle of his bat. He was getting frustrated and the next thing you know he was banging on it again. He looked up at me and said, 'Don't worry. This is how I fix my car.'" If Hayes has a bad at-bat, he goes to his first-base position at the start of the next inning and fires the practice ball at the far end of the dugout, says teammate Don Carman. "If he's had a good at-bat, he'll flip the practice ball softly to someone in the dugout."

Larry Bowa, Padres manager—During his first two weeks at the helm in 1987, he twice blew up in front of his players, once breaking some fungo bats and another time repeatedly kicking a trash can. "He threw some baseballs around in the clubhouse in anger and they were flying like shrapnel," said Tim Flannery. "I got into my locker like I was getting into a fox hole so I wouldn't get hit."

Mark Portugal, Twins—When Portugal was pulled in a 1987 game, recalls teammate Steve Lombardozzi, "Mark tried to kick a trash basket and missed it and flipped himself so that he landed square on his back."

Jim Deshaies, Astros—Deshaies said he was ticked off after getting the hook during a 1986 game in Los Angeles, but he couldn't stay mad because of an unexpected event. "I was kicking up a storm and I fired my glove into my locker and all of a sudden I heard, 'Hee, hee, ha, ha!' I looked around and realized that my glove had hit and set off a laughing box that I have. All I could do was laugh."

Joe Magrane, Cardinals—He was so upset after making an out that he flung his bat into the dugout where it hit trainer Gene Gieselmann in the shoulder. Sounding slightly less than contrite, Magrane said, "If it's going to hit anybody, it should hit Gene because he can treat himself." Another of Magrane's out-of-control releases bounced off the railing in front of the Cardinals dugout. "That's got to be exciting for the people sitting behind the dugout." Magrane said. "Here they are, bringing back their hotdogs and their beers, not really seeing what's going on. It's a great way to help fan interest.

And as for the people in the dugout—what fun is it to come to the ball park and just chew seeds?"

Tony Fernandez, Blue Jays: "Tony had just been retired by [veteran knuckleballer] Phil Niekro for the third consecutive time," recalls teammate Mark Eichhorn. "So Tony ran into the dugout, threw his helmet down in disgust, and ran back into the tunnel. We could hear him yell, 'Go home, old man! Go home and tend to your grandchildren! Leave this game for the young kids!' "

▲

COOL SNAP

Tigers catcher Mike Heath is still remembered in the minors for one of the all-time great snaps.

"It happened in 1979 in Tucson," recalled Ed Lynch of the Cubs. "Mike had a terrible game and afterward I saw him systematically destroy the team's soda machine. It wasn't like he got a bat and whaled on it until he cooled down. He took his time and used a screwdriver. After he got enough screws loose, he picked up his bat and wham! The front of the machine fell off. Then Mike picked up his screwdriver, loosened more screws, put his tool down, grabbed his bat, and bam! Another part of the machine fell off. I was amazed at how a guy could have a tantrum and be so systematic."

▲

REDEMPTION

Even though players understand that errors are part of the game, few can quickly shake off the awful feeling of committing a critical miscue. Some players throw tantrums. Others pray.

Mets third baseman Ray Knight plunged into despair during the sixth game of the 1986 World Series. "We were tied in the seventh inning and Boston had a runner on second when Jim Rice hit a routine grounder to me," Knight recalls. "But I threw the ball away and a batter later they scored the go-ahead run.

"I had never felt more devastated. Here we were trailing three games to two and I had just helped the Red Sox take the lead in the most critical game of my life. I went into the dugout after the inning and it was like all the blood had gone from my heart to my feet.

"I can't describe how terrible I felt. It was almost a suicidal feeling. I sat down on the bench and prayed. I said, 'Dear Lord, if there is any justice in this game, give me the chance to redeem myself.' I didn't ask for success. I just wanted a chance to redeem myself for that error. Fortunately, in the bottom of the tenth, I got a hit to drive in a run and then I scored the winning run. After the game I went into the locker room and said a long prayer of thanks."

 ## WHAT DO PLAYERS HATE MOST ABOUT SITTING IN THE DUGOUT?

1. **Getting hit with spit from tobacco chewers**
2. **Watching tobacco chewers dribble on themselves**
3. **Stepping in pools of spit and chewed-up tobacco**

If the majority of players had their way, tobacco chewing would be outlawed in the dugout. According to the *Baseball Confidential* survey, no habit is more despised than tobacco chewing and spitting. Yet the tradition continues, albeit in ever-shrinking numbers.

"I don't understand why they do it," says Don Carman of the Phillies. "It's a terrible habit. Tobacco juice drips down their face, gets on their uniform and all over their hands. The worst is [teammate] Rick Schu. We call him Doctor Dirt."

Some players stick a chaw in their jaw as routinely as they don their uniform. "Donnie Hill [of the White Sox] always has to chew tobacco," says teammate Ozzie Guillen. "I think he chews even when he sleeps. I asked him once, 'When you make love with your wife, do you chew tobacco?' And he said, 'I think so.' "

Anti-chaw players claim they wouldn't mind quite so much if the tobacco chewers wouldn't spit on them. "When Fred Lynn [of the

Orioles] isn't playing, he's kind of a pain in the neck because then he chews in the dugout," says teammate Mike Flanagan. "And when he chews, he tries to spit on new shoes. I always check the lineup to see if he's playing. If's he's not, I make sure I wear old shoes."

Lynn might qualify as a spitting image of former Padres star pitcher Randy Jones. Says Gary Lucas of the Angels, "I never met a spitter quite like Randy. When we played for San Diego, we wore white shoes and Randy thought nothing of coming up and decorating our shoes with tobacco juice. Once he went up to Rollie Fingers in the dugout and said, 'Rollie, I'm going to spit on your shoes.' Rollie said, 'No, that's boring.' So Randy spit right into Rollie's ear."

The major leagues don't have as many accurate spitters as they used to. It's not like the good old days, laments Tigers coach Billy Consolo. "In the 1950s, tobacco chewers were fellas who could hit another guy's sanitary socks or shoes. You got points for that. But today most chewers spit straight down. It gets so messy that now dugouts have to be hosed down." Consolo claims that Darrell Evans of the Tigers is among the sloppiest tobacco chewers in the league. "He's a shredder. He chews it until it's almost like sawdust, and when he flops it out, it's all over the dugout floor."

Consolo should talk, says Darnell Coles of the Tigers. "As a tobacco chewer, he's absolutely nauseating. He has a habit of dribbling on himself and swallowing some of it. A half hour after he starts chewing, he drinks a bottle of Maalox for his stomach. Yet he still crams the chew in his mouth."

Some of the Cubs were glad to see manager Jim Frey get fired in 1986. Not that he was a bad manager—it was just that he was a gross tobacco chewer, claimed one player. "He was always gagging and spitting up." Who can forget the time Frey swallowed some tobacco juice in the middle of a live interview with Harry Caray on his pregame radio show? Certainly not the tens of thousands of listeners who heard Frey gagging and coughing up his chew.

Milt Thompson of the Phillies says he can stomach most anything that tobacco chewers do because he's seen it all. "No one was more disgusting than this one manager I had in the minors. He'd stick a couple of chews in his mouth and pretty soon he'd gag and throw up his chews. Then he'd catch them in his hand . . . and put them back in his mouth. Is that gross or what?"

HARD TO SWALLOW

Pete Rose says his first experience with tobacco chewing was stomach-churning. When Rose broke in with the Reds, manager Fred Hutchinson told him to mix the chew with gum. "I told him I still wasn't feeling well, and Hutch asked me where the juice was. I said, 'What juice?'"

WHO IS THE SMARTEST MANAGER IN BASEBALL?

1. **Gene Mauch**
2. **Whitey Herzog**
3. **Dave Johnson**
4. **Chuck Tanner**

To hear the players tell it, Angels skipper Gene Mauch could have written the rule book himself; he's that knowledgeable. Even his critics will admit that he's the game's most astute field general.

"Mauch knows the rules better than anybody," declares Kirk Gibson of the Tigers. "He actually earned a run for the Angels against us because he cited some obscure rule." It happened during a game in 1987 when the Angels had runners on first and second. A pitch in the dirt bounced off the glove of catcher Mike Heath, who tried to retrieve the ball with his mask. Mauch promptly marched out of the dugout and called the umpire's attention to rarely invoked Rule 7.05 (d) which says it is an infraction if a fielder "deliberately touches a thrown ball with his cap, mask, or any part of his uniform detached from its proper place on his person." The umpires agreed with Mauch and awarded the runners two bases, giving the Angels a run. "To be quite honest," admitted Gibson, "we didn't know what was going on. But we do now."

Don Baylor, who played under Mauch in California, says that Mauch spends hours just studying his own team. "During BP, Mauch often stands behind the screen out near second base, not saying anything, just watching his hitters. He has a great knack for positioning his hot hitters in the lineup so the right guy gets up at the right time."

Also held in high esteem by players in both leagues for his baseball smarts is Whitey Herzog of the Cardinals. Few managers can match his overall experience; Herzog has worked in all phases of the game as a player, scout, farm director, manager, and general manager. "Whitey can take a team with medium or slightly above-average ability and turn them into a champion," says Kent Tekulve of the Phillies. "He knows how to use players in the right situations and how to get the most out of his team." Adds Tim Raines of the Expos, "He's so smart. He plays the type of game that is suited to his players and he seems to always come up a winner."

With each passing year, Davey Johnson of the Mets gains more respect from players. "He's got a sharp mind and is an eighties-type manager," said a Cub. "He knows how to handle today's players, he knows how to outfox opposing managers, and he knows how to use a computer to help him win." Says Mets coach Mel Stottlemyre, "What makes Davey so smart is the way he makes those great moves late in the game. Davey tries to make the other manager fall into certain traps. For example, he'll have one of the Met relievers warm up—even though he has no intention of using him in the game—to keep the other manager from using one of his pinch hitters."

When it comes to preparing for a game, Chuck Tanner of the Braves is near the top, according to the *Baseball Confidential* survey. Players cited Tanner's strong work ethic—such as getting to the ball park at noon for a night game. "He's the most prepared manager I've ever known," says Braves hurler Rick Mahler. "He's got baseball down to a science. He studies the other team in such detail that he is never surprised. He really concentrates on the little things of the game."

WHICH MANAGERS WOULD PLAYERS MOST AND LEAST LIKE TO PLAY FOR?

Most:	**Least:**
1. **Whitey Herzog**	1. **Dick Williams**
2. **Chuck Tanner**	2. **Gene Mauch**
	3. **Tommy Lasorda**

By far, the two skippers players would most like to play for are Whitey Herzog of the Cardinals and Chuck Tanner of the Braves. Here are some representative comments from players:

"We all know Herzog is going to manage a good game every time and he's not going to get outfoxed."

"The players on his team really like Herzog and the rest of us respect him."

"Players enjoy playing for Tanner because he's smart and he's a positive guy and keeps your confidence up."

"You can talk to Chuck about anything and you know where you stand. He also makes the game fun."

When the players were asked which manager they would least like to play for, Dick Williams of the Mariners took top dishonors, followed by Gene Mauch of the Angels and Tommy Lasorda of the Dodgers. Some players' remarks:

"When Williams left the Padres and took over the Mariners, 24 guys in San Diego were happily jumping up and down—that should tell you something about Williams."

"There's an abrasive, cavalier attitude about Dick Williams that makes players dislike him intensely."

"Mauch is tough to play for because he makes too many changes and seldom has a set lineup. It's frustrating for players when they don't know if they're starting the next day or not."

"Lasorda isn't very well liked because of his phoniness and Hollywood attitude."

"Lasorda is good for some laughs, but that gets old quick when you've been losing as often as he has. He also gets outmanaged more than most managers do."

Then there's this view from Charlie Kerfeld of the Astros, who says he wouldn't want to play for the hug-happy Lasorda because "every time I'd save a game, he'd want to come out to the mound and make out with me. I couldn't handle that—not with him."

HOW MANAGERS TRY TO "HELP" UMPIRES

In looking for that little extra edge, managers plant "seeds" in the minds of umpires, hoping to get them to make a favorable call. The skippers do this from the dugout by either badgering the men in blue or by pointing out some alleged infraction committed by the opposition.

Joe Sambito of the Red Sox explains how his manager, John McNamara, uses the latter approach:

"Ellis Burks [of the Red Sox] led off with a single and McNamara yelled at home plate umpire Rocky Roe to watch out for [Royals pitcher] Charlie Liebrandt's pickoff move. McNamara told Roe, 'Hey, he's got a different move toward first. Watch him. He's not stepping toward first.' By warning the umpire of what might happen, the ump will be looking for it. Every time Liebrandt threw over to first, McNamara kept yelling balk, trying to get Rocky Roe to call it. We kept hoping that if Liebrandt came close to committing the infraction, maybe Roe would call it on him."

Tony Gwynn of the Padres says his manager, Larry Bowa, likes to work on the umpire just before the game begins. "It's important to get the umpire to think your way. We were playing the Pirates a few weeks ago and Larry went out before the game to ask [home plate umpire] Bob Engel to watch this certain pitcher who has a habit of going to his mouth and walking off the mound. If a pitcher goes to his mouth while he's still on the mound, then it's a balk. During the game, the pitcher walked almost off the mound, but had one foot on it and went to his mouth. Larry started yelling at Engel to call a balk but Engel wouldn't do it. It was Larry's way to try and sneak a call. Sometimes it works and you end up scoring the winning run that way."

Many managers like to get on the home plate umpire early if he's not calling the borderline pitches in their favor. "Buck Rodgers [of the Expos] needles them pretty good," says Wallace Johnson. "The first pitch of the game might be a little low and Buck will think it should be a strike and he'll start complaining right away to get the ump to make those calls."

Tommy Lasorda of the Dodgers also jumps on umps early. Says one of his former players, Jerry Royster of the White Sox, "I always knew when Tommy was going to leave the dugout for an argument with the ump. He would put a chew in his mouth and then run out. If the argument got a little ugly, Tommy would get real close to the ump and then let some of that tobacco juice fly out of the side of his mouth."

▲

MANAGERS BEST AT INFLUENCING UMPIRES

1. Whitey Herzog
2. Sparky Anderson
3. Chuck Tanner
4. Gene Mauch
5. Dick Williams

▲

WHERE IT'S AT

American League umpire Rocky Roe admits he doesn't always get in the last word on a questioned pitch.

He said that during a game in 1985, Tigers manager Sparky Anderson was harping over the way Roe called a pitch. "Rock, where was that pitch at?" Sparky demanded.

Roe said he turned to Sparky and declared, "You're a great manager, Sparky. You have the possibilities of a dynasty here. I really think I could like you personally too. But don't you know you don't end a sentence with the preposition 'at'?"

According to Roe, Anderson replied, "Well, then, where was that pitch at, dipstick?"

THE LOST ART OF BENCH JOCKEYING

"You couldn't break a chandelier if you took batting practice in a hotel lobby!" . . . "If a bird had your brains, he'd fly backward!" . . . "You're so fat, you have to shower in a car wash!"

Shouting zingers from the dugout at opposing pitchers and batters—once a common and accepted practice in the majors—has become as rare as a triple play.

"Bench jockeying is all but dead," declares Jerry Royster of the White Sox. "Players don't do it anymore because they think it's showing up the other team. Oh, sure, there are still a few individuals doing it, but if you jockey the opposing team now, you get strange looks from your own players."

It's happened more than once to Tom Browning of the Reds. "I was 'motherfucking' the umpire and [teammate] Tom Foley asked me, 'Why are you so loud?' And I said, 'Fuck you, Foley. I can do this all I want.' But not too many of us do anymore." Adds Ed Lynch of the Cubs, "Nowadays, if you come up with a good line and blast somebody, your teammates tell you, 'Jeez, you're mean. Sit down.' "

In years past, each team had a couple of players who would sit on the bench and ride every player who stepped up to the plate or on the pitcher's mound, said veteran Rick Manning of the Brewers. "Billy Martin was a great bench jockey. He used to scream at me all the time from the dugout. But times have changed. We've got too many quiet guys now."

One reason for the silence, says Dan Quisenberry of the Royals, is that today's ballplayer has more class. "Also, we all know that every dog has his day. And if you get on a guy too much, he's going to get you one way or another."

Teammate Frank White says that the role of the reserve player no longer includes jockeying opposing pitchers and batters to break their concentration. "Today, everybody gets along because so many have the same agent. Guys hang around the batting cage and talk to each other. Everybody goes out to dinner with friends on the other team. So players don't hate each other as much as players used to. A good bench jockey is a guy who just doesn't care about anybody else and yells loud enough for the opposition to hear him."

Although bench jockeys aren't extinct, they are an endangered species. Cubs hurler Rick Sutcliffe continues to verbally vex the opposition. "He can run his mouth with the best of them," says former teammate George Frazier of the Twins. "Against Philly, he was getting on [relief pitcher] Al Holland, saying how fat he was and how he couldn't get anyone out, that he couldn't throw hard and that we'd rip him good. Holland called time and then turned to our dugout and asked Sutcliffe if he wanted to fight. Sutcliffe started out of the dugout but the umps stepped in and told him to shut up. But he served his purpose. He got Holland rattled."

When 225-pound Charlie Kerfeld of the Astros faced the Mets for the first time, said former teammate Bill Dawley of the Cardinals, "The Mets kept yelling at him, 'Hey, it's John Candy on the mound!' "

Targets of bench jockeying are often players who are considered hotdogs. "We think Tracy Jones [of the Reds] acts too cool for school," says a Brave. "And we let him know it. There was a game when Ted Simmons hollered from our dugout, 'I'm on the field with Tracy Fucking Jones! Wait till I tell my dad. He ain't gonna believe it!' "

Kirk Gibson of the Tigers has a way of getting under the pitcher's skin, says a teammate. "He's always screaming at the pitcher, calling him a wimp or saying he's too chicken to throw a fastball."

Tom Paciorek of the Rangers says that manager Bobby Valentine gets on opposing players "to the point where they want to strangle him." His bench jockeying is so vicious, adds a Ranger, that a Royals pitcher once asked manager Dick Howser if he could throw his next pitch into the dugout at Valentine.

"I think bench jockeying is good," declares Ed Lynch. "It should be a part of the game like it was 20 or 30 years ago when it was really cruel. I personally enjoy it. I like to dish it out and I can take it too. It's healthy and gets people fired up. Unfortunately, it's become a lost art."

WHO'S BEST AT STEALING COACHES' SIGNS?

1. **Joe Nossek**
2. **Roger Craig**
3. **Gene Mauch**
4. **Chuck Tanner**
5. **Frank Robinson**

Managers, coaches, and reserve players practice espionage and counterespionage from the shadows of the dugout.

In a typical major league game, the manager flashes signs to his third-base coach, who relays the message to the batter and any base runners. Meanwhile, across the diamond in the opposing dugout, the manager and other members of his team try to detect and decipher these signals to thwart an upcoming play.

While there might be four basic messages—take, steal, hit-and-run, and bunt—the third-base coach will go through dozens of signs that don't mean anything just to confuse the sign stealers. Intercepting and decoding the signals requires patience and dedication—and no one had more of it than Joe Nossek, former coach of the Indians, Royals, and White Sox. Players in the *Baseball Confidential* survey rated Nossek, now a scout, the best sign stealer of the 1980s.

Nossek says sign stealing is nothing more than educated guessing. "You watch the opposing third-base coach, and then check out the manager, and things start falling into place. For instance, say you've been watching a team the first two games of a series and it hasn't tried anything in the way of stealing or a hit-and-run, and then you suddenly pick up a whole new series of signs. You just assume the runner's going, and you call a pitchout."

Players whom Nossek coached over the years are still in awe over his sign-stealing prowess. "Nossek was the best I've ever seen," says Rick Manning of the Brewers. "I played with him for five years at Cleveland and he was excellent. One year he called for pitchouts about 18 times and we got those guys more often than not. Sometimes he'd pick up their signs as early as the first inning. Sometimes it took a whole game. But I'll tell you what. Before that series was over, he'd have their signs."

Bill Schroeder of the Brewers remembers a game when Nossek decoded their signs. "Every time we would try to hit-and-run or steal, they pitched out. We ended up having to change our signs." That's considered a victory for the sign stealer. "Once you get a team changing signs, then you've got them thinking and in a state of confusion," said Manning.

Nossek turned to technology to help him swipe signs. "He actually had someone videotape the opposing coaches and managers," recalls Ron Kittle of the Yankees. "He'd study the video and review the signs. He was so clever at it."

Today the master of this arcane trade is Roger Craig, manager of the Giants. "Roger is outstanding," declares Tigers skipper Sparky Anderson, whom Craig coached under before taking over the Giants in 1985. "For 2½ hours every game, he involves himself with his eyes. He's always watching what the other manager is doing in the dugout."

Tigers coach Billy Consolo said that in all his years in baseball, he never saw a better sign stealer than Craig. "He is an absolute student of watching the managers and coaches on the other side. And, by God, if you give Roger enough time, he's got you."

When Craig was a coach in Detroit, he tape-recorded his observations rather than committing them to memory. He knew that, in general, a team's signs follow the same pattern throughout the year. Over time, Craig built up a pretty good book on the opposition.

"He just has a natural instinct for stealing signs," says Kirk Gibson of the Tigers. "It was almost a joke when he was with us. We'd have the other team's signs and know what they were up to. In 1984, when the Tigers won the world championship, he had a really amazing percentage for calling pitchouts at the right time."

Although managers and coaches often get the blame for having their signs stolen, Craig says the players are most often the guilty ones. "When a play is on, the base runners will try to set up differently and they tip it off," he said. "I get some [tipoffs] from the runners, the first- and third-base coaches, the managers, or sometimes I play a hunch."

Since many of the modern stadiums have wide-open dugouts that face each other, it's difficult for a manager to conceal his signals from the likes of two other top-flight sign stealers, Angels manager Gene Mauch and Braves pilot Chuck Tanner. Mauch and Tanner are so good at their craft, say players, that opposing managers sometimes go into the dugout tunnel to give signals away from their prying eyes. The two field generals have not only fine-tuned the art of sign stealing but also of sign flashing. They thwart sign stealers by using decoys. Instead of signaling the third-base coach directly, Mauch and Tanner will go through a series of meaningless signs while a coach or a reserve player in the dugout flashes the real signs to the third-base coach.

Players often marvel at the patience of sign stealer Frank Robinson, a coach with the Orioles. He spends most of the game just staring at either the opposing manager or the opposing third-base coach. "It's a very boring thing to do," says Mike Flanagan of the Orioles, "but it's a very important thing to do. Obviously, he's very good at it because he's helped us many times."

Many of the reserves use their time on the bench learning the art of sign stealing. Yankees reserve infielder Mike Fischlin uses a little tape recorder in the dugout as he spies on the opposing manager and third-base coach, says teammate Dennis Rasmussen. "He's very good at it. He tries to pick up something and work out patterns. He'll talk into the tape recorder and say, 'Left hand to ear, right hand to chest' and then see if any play is on."

SIGN OF THE TIMES

When Mariners manager Dick Williams was asked, "Do your players miss signs because the signals are too complicated?" Williams replied, "If they were any simpler, I'd be using flash cards."

HOW RESERVES HELP WIN GAMES FROM THE BENCH

Players can help a team win even when they aren't in the lineup. Most reserves don't just sit on the bench and mindlessly watch the game. Rather, they often study the opposing pitcher and catcher, looking for a clue that might tip them off to what pitch is coming.

Says Tony Gwynn of the Padres, "Former starters who now sit on the bench aren't accustomed to being there and it can be hard on them. They think, 'God, I should be out there.' Yet someone like Puff [Graig Nettles] could sit there and make the most of the situation. He'd look at a pitcher and know from the way the pitcher gripped the ball in his glove what was coming. Puff was great at spotting little things like that and relaying them to the rest of us. I guess when you've been around that long, you learn new ways to contribute to the team."

Nettles, who's now with the Braves, is so observant that "after an inning or two he almost always will spot something about the opposing pitcher's delivery," says a teammate. "Graig will say something like, 'Hey, he's got one eye closed, it's a curveball.' Or, 'His mitt is closer to his body, it's a fastball.' "

The studious benchwarmers closely watch not only the way a hurler pitches but also the way a catcher sets up behind the plate, explains Expos reserve outfielder Herm Winningham. He says he and teammate Wallace Johnson sit at the end of the bench and spend most of their time with their eyes locked on the opposing catcher. "We can sometimes tell the location of the pitch beforehand and pass it on to the batter."

Even regulars study the opposing pitcher from the dugout while waiting their turn at bat. Pat Tabler of the Indians "is always trying to find some little idiosyncrasy in the pitcher—whether he's holding the ball cross-seams or with the seams or showing a lot of white," says teammate Tom Candiotti.

Indians hurler Doug Jones, who pitched briefly for the Brewers in their pennant-winning season in 1982, recalls that Milwaukee stars Robin Yount and Jim Gantner "used to have a contest to see who would pick up something first. Once or twice they ran bets—and they set the stakes pretty high."

RBI'S—RATS BATTED IN

When a rat ran into the Twins' dugout during a 1986 game at Cleveland, pitcher Bert Blyleven took a bat and looked like he was going to pummel the rodent. But Blyleven had second thoughts. "I remembered what happened to Dave Winfield and I didn't want to spend the night in jail," he said. (Winfield's warm-up throw hit a seagull and killed it during a 1983 game in Toronto.)

Nevertheless, the rat met a similar fate. "Blyleven cornered the rat," recalled teammate Tom Brunansky, "and when the rat tried to bite [Twins outfielder] Mickey Hatcher, Mickey took the bat and bashed it to death."

THE PITCHER'S MOUND

WHAT DO PLAYERS SAY WHEN
THEY HOLD A CONFERENCE
ON THE PITCHER'S MOUND?

Whenever a manager, infielder, or catcher goes to the mound for a confab with the pitcher, they usually discuss strategy: setting the defense, deciding what to throw the hitter, determining if the hurler is tired. But often the conversation isn't as serious as you think. Here's a sampling, gleaned from the *Basball Confidential* survey, of what they *really* say out there:

Between Pitchers and Managers

George Brett, Royals: "On Opening Day, 1987, which was Billy Gardner's first day as our manager, he went to the mound to take out starter Danny Jackson. He got the ball from Danny and said, 'Thataway to ruin my debut.' "

Gene Nelson, Athletics: "In 1986 when I was with the White Sox and Jim Fregosi had just taken over as manager, he called me in from the bullpen with the bases loaded and no outs. I expected to hear the typical routine of how to pitch to the batter and all that. Instead, Fregosi said, 'I'm going to give you a chore. Try to get out of this one.' He handed me the ball and walked off. I got out of it. A few days later, I was brought in with runners on second and third and one out. All Fregosi said to me was, 'Here, it's easier now.' I got out of it. Then in the next game, I came in with the bases loaded and no outs. Fregosi just said one sentence: 'See, with all this experience, it's a lot easier for you.' He gave me the ball and I proceeded to give up three runs."

Mike Flanagan, Orioles: "It was one of those spring-training games where if they hit it on the ground, we made an error and if they hit it in the air, we couldn't see it because the sun was so bright. So Earl Weaver came out to the mound and told me, 'Don't let them hit it on the ground and don't let them hit it in the air either.' So on the next pitch, Juan Samuel [of the Phillies] hit a line drive right to the second baseman for a double play to get me out of the inning and Earl said, 'Boy, what a genius I am!' "

Mel Stottlemyre, Mets coach: "[Reliever] Doug Sisk had runners on the corners of a tight game and I went out to the mound and said something really basic like, 'If the ball is hit back to you and you don't think you can get two, check the runner at third and throw to first.' And he said, 'You don't have to think of anything else to say. I know what you're doing. You're stalling for time so Jesse [Orosco] can get more time to warm up.' I almost broke up right there."

Scott McGregor, Orioles: "I was getting knocked around pretty good in Boston and I gave up a grand slam to Wade Boggs. [Baltimore manager] Cal Ripkin came out and said, 'If you know any tricks, this would be a good time to start.' So I went ahead and gave up another home run."

Rick Rhoden, Yankees: "One time when I was with the Dodgers, Tommy Lasorda went out to the mound for a pitching change. He had two relievers warming up, but the one he wanted to bring in wasn't ready yet. Since it was Lasorda's second trip to the mound in the inning, he had to make a move. So he stalled for time. He waited for the umpire to come out to the mound. The ump said, 'Who do you want to bring in?' Lasorda then asked him, 'Who would you bring in?' The ump said it wasn't his decision and Lasorda kept saying, 'Well, what should I do?' The ump demanded that Lasorda make up his mind and they began arguing. By the time they finished, the reliever was ready. The ump asked again, 'Who do you want?' Lasorda asked him, 'Who would you bring in?' Finally, the ump said, 'The righthander.' And Lasorda said, 'Then bring in the lefthander.' "

Between Pitchers and Infielders

Scott McGregor: "Our second baseman, Rich Dauer, once called time and walked to the mound and told me, 'I don't know why I'm here. They told me to come in here, but I'm not going to tell you anything that you don't already know. They wanted me to come in here, so I came in here and now I'm going to go back, okay?' And he went back."

Mark Gubicza, Royals: "George Brett will come over to me and say, 'Gubie, why are you pitching this guy so carefully? He told me he hates facing you. Just throw the ball down the middle.' Or sometimes, if I'm in a jam, George will try and psych me up by saying, 'You stink!' "

Tom Henke, Blue Jays fastball pitcher: "After I'd given up six runs in a game against Baltimore, [shortstop] Tony Fernandez came in and told me, 'Hey, Tom, don't throw any more fastballs.' "

Bill Dawley, Cardinals: "When I was with the Astros, I took the mound for my 60th appearance of the year. Our second baseman, Bill Doran knew I had an incentive clause that gave me a bonus for appearing in at least 60 games. I was just about to throw my first pitch when he called time, came over, and said, 'Hey, Bill, you're $45,000 richer.' Then he turned around and went back to his position."

Mark Clear, Brewers: "I was pitching for the Angels and it was late in the game and I was in some trouble. I had given up a few hits and a run and I was working slow out there. [Second baseman] Bobby Grich called time and walked up to me and said, 'Do you see that blonde over there behind the dugout?' I looked over there and saw her and nodded my head. Grich then said, 'Well, I've got a date with her tonight, so would you please hurry up?' "

Between Pitchers and Catchers
Scott Bailes, Indians: "When Andy Allanson catches me and I give up a home run, he walks out to the mound and says, 'C'mon, throw the next pitch. They can't hit it any harder than that last one.' "

Paul Mirabella, Brewers southpaw: "In my major league debut, I pitched against the White Sox. My first pitch sailed 40 feet over the head of my catcher, John Ellis, and hit the screen. John called time and came out to the mound and asked, 'Are you nervous?' And I said, 'Yeah, just a little.' And he said, 'There's nothing to be nervous about. We haven't beaten Chicago all year and they kick the hell out of lefthanders.' Then he turned around and walked back to the plate."

Terry Kennedy, Orioles: "I was catching Tim Lollar when we were with the Padres, and in a game against Philadelphia, he gave up back-to-back monster homers that landed in the upper deck about five feet apart. When I went out to the mound, Lollar was still staring at the upper deck and he started laughing because the balls were hit so hard. I began to laugh too, and said, 'At least when you give up homers, you give up memorable ones.' Then [manager] Dick Williams came out and Lollar said, 'I bet you didn't think I could throw hard enough for them to be hit that far, did you?' I kept my mask on and put my glove in front of my face because I was laughing so hard."

Floyd Rayford, Orioles: "I remember catching Sammy Stewart and we had a 3–0 count on Dave Kingman with the bases loaded. I put down a fastball and Sammy shook it off. I put down another fastball and he shook it off again. So I walked out to the mound and said, 'Sammy, what are we going to do?' He said, 'Let's go with the hard slider.' On my way back to the plate, I felt it was the wrong pitch, so I called for the fastball but he shook me off. Finally, I put down the slider. Sammy threw it and Kingman hit it for a grand slam. I went back to the mound and before I could say anything Sammy said, 'You should have called for the fastball.' "

WHAT TACTICS DO PITCHERS USE TO PSYCH OUT BATTERS?

In an attempt to gain the edge over batters, pitchers sometimes play head games with them.

Hurlers such as Charlie Kerfeld of the Astros, Sammy Stewart of the Indians, and Joaquin Andujar of the Athletics deliberately try to make hitters question their sanity.

For example, Kerfeld makes himself look like a slob. "I like to chew tobacco and see how dirty I can get my uniform," he explains. "I spit all over myself. When I come into the game, batters say, 'Hey, look at that hog with spit all over him. He can't get anybody out.' That's what I want them to think." Kerfeld believes it's easier to get out batters who underestimate him.

A little imagination on the mound can sometimes rattle a batter. Mike Boddicker of the Orioles marvels at the time when Stewart, a righthander, decided to pitch lefthanded to Dave Revering during a crucial moment in a one-run game. "It was unbelievable," said Boddicker. "Sammy turned around on the mound and came set with the ball in his left hand. Revering quickly called time out. It really messed him up. Sammy got him out on the next pitch—throwing righthanded."

Andujar loves to make batters believe he's crazy out on the mound, claims Bobby Meacham of the Yankees. "He throws behind you or over your head. Sometimes batters try to think along with the pitcher, but if you think he's crazy out there, you can't figure out what he's going to do."

That's the whole idea, says Al Hrabosky, a former relief ace who has coached several Cardinal relievers. Hrabosky, who turned the mound into a stage for his "Mad Hungarian" foot-stomping, glove-pounding routine between pitches, said when he hit a bad streak, "I spread a few more rumors about my sanity—or lack of it."

Spreading rumors about scuffing baseballs can also screw up batters. "I think the best pitchers at psyching out batters are the guys who have been accused of doctoring the ball," said an All-Star hurler. "I'm talking about pitchers like Mike Scott, Dave Smith, and Rick Rhoden. Once the hitter thinks the pitcher is cheating, he's psyched out to begin with."

An entire team—the Mets—has been totally unnerved by Scott and his scuffball reputation, claims Cardinals manager Whitey Herzog. "Scott has got the Mets' number. They are so psyched out because they are too worried about his doctored pitches." When a batter frets over scuffed balls, says Bill Madlock, "the pitcher will get him out with another pitch that the batter normally would have hit if he hadn't been concentrating on doctored balls."

Some pitchers toy with hitters' minds by lousing up their timing. For example, says Mets coach Mel Stottlemyre, "Rick Sutcliffe [of the Cubs] waits a long time between pitches and is very slow and deliberate. Then at other times, he'll try to throw a pitch before the batter is ready. That's his way of psyching out hitters."

Gene Garber of the Braves annoys batters by making them cool their heels at the plate, says a teammate. "He'll step on and off the rubber, throw over to first base again and again, and repeatedly shake off signs. This can be upsetting to the batter and make him antsy."

Nolan Ryan takes a tad bit longer than normal between pitches just to give the batter more time to think about facing his 95-mile-per-hour fastball, says batting champion Tony Gwynn. "Nolan knows he throws 95, and the batter knows he throws 95. Nolan is going to take his sweet time and nobody is going to say anything about it because he's Nolan Ryan."

To make things even tougher on batters, Ryan has perfected a subtle yet intimidating psych-out tactic—the long, cold stare. "He has this stare that gets to batters," says Pirates coach Ray Miller. "Usually, if a young guy hits the ball hard off Nolan, the kid will get the stare when he's in the on-deck circle for his next at-bat. Nolan will step off the rubber, rub up the ball, and stare directly at the kid. The kid starts thinking, 'What's he going to do to me?' "

Gary Redus of the White Sox learned in his rookie year not to make light of Ryan's stare. "In a late-season game, we had a lot of rookies in the lineup and we were hitting cheap singles off Ryan and stealing bases. I stole one and was on third when he gave me that stare. I started laughing and then said, 'I'm sorry. I won't do that again.' He didn't say a word. On the very next pitch, he hit the batter, Dave Van Gorder, with a fastball."

The Reds' young reliever Rob Murphy wishes more hurlers could lay an "eye-lock" on hitters. He's still in awe over the stare that Ryan gave Cincinnati's Eric Davis after Davis belted a homer against him in 1987. "Nolan walked toward home plate and waited for Davis to trot by him. Nolan just gave him that long stare. I said to myself, 'Damn, I'd like to do that to a hitter'—but I'm no Nolan Ryan."

Although many pitchers try to use the stare tactic, few can actually pull it off. "Dave Stieb [of the Blue Jays] stares at you whenever you get a hit off him, no matter who you are," says Marty Barrett of the Red Sox. "It's silly because it makes hitters become more aggressive against him. That's why everybody bears down when they face him."

Tim Raines of the Expos cites Bob Welch of the Dodgers and Bill Gullickson of the Reds as hurlers who glower at batters whenever they get a hit. "If a guy gets a homer, Gullickson sometimes follows the batter with his eyes around the bases," said Raines.

Oil Can Boyd of the Red Sox has tried the cold stare with mixed results. "Maybe it's worked for him in the past," said DeWayne Buice of the Angels. "But when he gave us that stare, it failed. He got a 10-

minute 'lube job.' He gave up four runs in two-thirds of an inning and was gone."

DON'T GET MAD, GET EVEN

For fast-working pitchers whose rhythm gets disrupted by batters who take their sweet time getting set, Angels broadcaster Ken Brett has a solution that worked for him when he was a pitcher.

Brett's nemesis was Mike Hargrove, first baseman for the Rangers and Indians, who, until he retired in 1985, made pitchers seethe because he took forever to get ready in the batter's box. "He had this long routine every time," recalls Brett. "Mike would fix his jersey, rub his thumb, adjust his helmet, fix his jersey again, and on and on.

"I was a fast worker and I didn't want to bother with him. I figured he'd get a hit off me anyway so I threw him a fastball right in the stomach—and I felt so good about it."

 WHICH PITCHERS STRIKE THE MOST FEAR IN BATTERS' HEARTS?

1. **Nolan Ryan**
2. **Lee Smith**
3. **Mitch Williams**
4. **Roger Clemens**
5. **Mark Langston**
6. **Bobby Witt**

Batters may not want to admit it, but a few fireballing pitchers literally inspire fear at the plate. Players say they aren't so much afraid of getting hit as they are of looking bad by striking out.

According to the *Baseball Confidential* survey, all-time major league strikeout leader Nolan Ryan—even though he's over 40—still scares the hell out of batters. "Nolan has more effect on a team than any other opposing pitcher," declares Cardinals manager Whitey Herzog. "That's because the players think about facing him the day before he pitches, the day he pitches, and the day after he pitches. On Monday they say, 'Oh shit, Ryan is pitching on Tuesday.' On Tuesday they say, 'Oh, shit, look at his fastball.' And on Wednesday they say, 'Wow, did you see how fast he was?'"

Says Barry Larkin of the Reds, "When you're a kid coming up, everybody tells you how hard Ryan throws. You go out there thinking the guy is seven feet tall and throws 800 miles per hour."

At the peak of Ryan's career, a strange phenomenon occurred in the opposing clubhouse—hitters suddenly complained of injuries and took themselves out of the lineup. "Every time Nolan pitched, somebody had a stiff neck, sore back, pulled muscle, or sprained ankle," said Frank White of the Royals.

Cubs relief ace Lee Smith (a.k.a. Lee "Iasmokah" by his team-mates) was named by many hitters as "the most fearsome figure on the mound." Combining his awesome size—6 feet, 6 inches and 220 pounds—with a fastball that has been clocked at 99 miles per hour, Smith is at his most terrifying at Wrigley Field. "You can't help but be a little scared when he takes the mound in the ninth inning of a game that started at three P.M. in Wrigley Field and he throws pure gas from out of the shadows," says an Astro. "He looks like he's throwing about 150 miles an hour and, as big as he is, you don't pick up the ball at all."

Smith's catcher, Jody Davis, says that even plate umpires some-times have bailed out when Smith uncorks one of his blazing fastballs out of the shadows. "I can sense them pull away," said Davis. "They're scared. They're only human." Davis admits that he some-times shies away too. "The shadows are killers. I can't see Lee's ball any better than the batter or the ump."

The Phillies often talk about how formidable Smith is, says Philadelphia beat writer Bill Brown. "Mike Schmidt said the ultimate baseball nightmare for him would be facing Lee Smith who's pitching out of the shadows after Andre Dawson had been beaned by a Phillies pitcher in the previous inning and Schmidt had already homered earlier in the game."

At least Ryan and Smith have a pretty good idea where their

pitches are going. What's even more frightening, admit batters, are wild fastball pitchers like lefty Mitch Williams and Bobby Witt, both of the Rangers. "It seems like they don't know where the ball is going," declares Bobby Meacham of the Yankees. "It's the erratic hard-throwing pitcher like Williams you fear the most," adds Butch Wynegar of the Angels. As a rookie in spring training in 1985, Williams was so feared because of his wildness that he wasn't allowed to throw to anyone batting lefthanded or wearing a uniform number under 50 (rostered players). Witt's control is so questionable that "hitters tend to tippy-toe to the plate rather than dig in," adds Paul Mirabella of the Brewers.

Also rated high as fear-provoking pitchers are strikeout artists Mark Langston of the Mariners and Roger Clemens of the Red Sox. "These guys have the ability to overpower batters and that tends to embarrass them," says Dan Plesac of the Brewers. "Let's face it. The big fear hitters have is striking out and looking bad. That's what these guys make them do."

Obviously, most hitters don't go up to the plate shaking in their spikes when they face these flame-throwers. "You can't be intimidated," says Wade Boggs of the Red Sox. "If you are, then it's time to get out of the game. Because once you're scared when you get into the box, you're not going to be that good of a hitter."

Teammate Jim Rice agrees. "When these pitchers are on a roll, they can sometimes be intimidating, but you can't let them know that," he says. "If you let them know they can intimidate you when you go up to the plate, you're 50 percent beaten already."

Kevin Seitzer of the Royals believes an apprehensive batter has no business being in the bigs. "I don't get intimidated because I think I can beat any pitcher. That's the attitude a hitter has to have in order to be successful. I believe that I have to be better than the guy on the mound and if he gets me out, then it's just because he's lucky."

THE LOWDOWN ON THE KNOCKDOWN

Almost to a man, pitchers swear they don't deliberately throw at a hitter to *hurt* him. However, under certain circumstances, they admit that they will throw *at* him.

There's a fine line between the knockdown and the brushback. The latter is good, hard-nosed baseball. When hitters dig in and crowd the plate, they try to stake their claim to the inside corner. Pitchers challenge this ownership by attempting to move the hitter off the plate with a tight, inside fastball. The knockdown serves a more sinister purpose—retribution. It's often thrown after a teammate has been dusted or a hitter has shown up the pitcher. No matter which pitch is thrown, it's dangerous. A 90-mile-an-hour-plus inside fastball reaches the hitter in about 4/10 of a second with an impact that can shatter his cheekbone, impair his vision, or actually kill him—all of which have happened in the majors.

"I don't think a pitcher should ever try to hurt a hitter," says Roger Clemens of the Red Sox. "But you have to pitch inside. A hitter must realize that a part of the plate is mine. And if he leans in too far, then I'm coming inside. That has to be done to be a successful pitcher."

Angels hurler Jack Lazorko says batters who notoriously crowd the plate, such as Don Baylor and Brian Downing, "know full well that we pitchers have to move them off the plate." (Baylor is painfully aware of that—he set the major league record for getting hit by a pitched ball for the 244th time midway in the 1987 season.) Yankee slugger Dave Winfield has hit the deck more than most batters, says teammate Wayne Tolleson. "He's a big man with a big swing and when a pitcher has to go inside, he wants to make sure it's tight and not make a mistake by giving him a pitch to pull."

Echoing the feelings of most batters, Mike Easler of the Yankees says, "It's all right to pitch inside—but low, not high. A pitcher has no right throwing at a guy's head."

Although no batters are secretly targeted for knockdown pitches, some hurlers contend they will fire a "purpose" pitch if provoked. Angels veteran catcher Butch Wynegar believes "there's only a certain breed of pitchers—a certain five percent—who are not afraid to knock somebody down and take the consequences."

Cocky players will eat more than their share of dirt, says Wallace Johnson of the Expos. "Pitchers don't like hotdogs like Len Dykstra [of the Mets] and Brett Butler [of the Indians]. Pitchers won't bean them, but they'll throw way up and in at those types of players."

Some pitchers will deliberately knock down a batter if they know it will upset him, says Mets coach Mel Stottlemyre. "Darryl Straw-berry gets very emotional and angry anytime there is a ball thrown inside to him. Some pitchers try to use that to break his concentra-tion."

If a batter ticks off a pitcher, he's going down. When Devon White of the Angels attempted to break up Royals pitcher Danny Jackson's no-hitter in 1986 by bunting, Jackson fired a "purpose" pitch at him. "If a guy's got a no-hitter going, you don't bunt," said Jackson, who finished with a two-hitter. "[Shortstop] Buddy Bilancalana came to me and said, 'He's got to go down.' He didn't have to tell me that. I already knew."

Pitchers will send a batter sprawling in retaliation for the knock-down of their teammate. For example, when Andre Dawson of the Cubs was beaned by Eric Show of the Padres in 1987, Chicago pitcher Scott Sanderson brushed back Tony Gwynn three times and threw at Chris Brown before being ejected. Gywnn, the 1987 National League batting champ, revealed that the game "was the first and only time in my life that I was scared to go to the plate."

Wynegar gives a vivid description of how the law of the baseball jungle works. "During a three-game series between the Twins and the Yankees, Reggie Jackson hit the ground three days in a row. The third time, Reggie turned to me—I was catching—and said, 'If I go down again, I'm coming after you!' The ump got between us to cool us down. On the next pitch, Reggie hit it 440 feet over the center-field fence. I led off the next inning and as Tom Underwood wound up, I thought, 'He's not going to hit me, is he?' He did. I stared at Underwood and he shrugged his shoulders as if to say he was ordered to drill me. I went to first base and looked at Reggie in right field. I tipped my helmet and he tipped his. We both understood how the game is played."

IT HURTS TO THINK ABOUT IT

Red Sox outfielder Don Baylor, who breaks his own major league record every time he gets hit by a pitch, says he harbors no malice toward the pitchers who have drilled him—except John Denny. The hurler, who played for the Cardinals, Indians, Phillies, and Reds, "was a headhunter," claims Baylor. "He was one of those guys I'd like to get—on or off the field, it doesn't matter. He tried to deliberately hurt people."

WHICH PITCHERS DOCTOR THE BALL?

Most Often Accused:
1. **Mike Scott**
2. **Rick Rhoden**
3. **Don Sutton**
4. **Dave Smith**
5. **Tommy John**
6. **Nolan Ryan**

Caught and Suspended:
1. **Kevin Gross**
2. **Joe Niekro**
3. **Rick Honeycutt**

Although players admit that cheating on the pitching mound has been a part of baseball for decades, they believe there's more skulduggery today than ever before.

Before retiring in 1983, 314-game winner Gaylord Perry did the most to advance the science of doctored balls. It took 21 years before Perry was caught slippery-handed in 1982. Today, three pitchers toil with the stigma of being labeled "convicted doctors." All were given 10-day suspensions. In 1980, umpires discovered Rick Honeycutt, then with the Mariners, had a thumbtack taped to the index finger of his glove hand. In 1987, arbiters caught Joe Niekro of the Twins with a piece of sandpaper and an emery board in his hip pocket during a game. A week later, Kevin Gross of the Phillies was found with sandpaper glued to his glove.

The threat of punishment hasn't deterred hurlers from flinging illegal balls, according to the *Baseball Confidential* survey. "Most everyone gets by with it," claims Whitey Herzog. "If I went out there and got my brains beat out, I'd be throwing them [doctored balls]."

Adds Herm Winningham of the Expos, "I think everybody doctors the ball at one time or another."

That's an overstatement, but some do it more than others. "Yeah, like the whole Houston pitching staff," declares Bill Madlock. The Astro hurlers most often accused are Mike Scott, Dave Smith, and Nolan Ryan. Opponents claim the trio throw "right-turn sliders"— fastballs that veer out of the strike zone because the balls are cut or scuffed.

"Those three have been doctoring the ball the last couple of years," admitted a Houston source who took part in the survey. "Scott does it with sandpaper. Leon Durham [of the Cubs] actually found sandpaper on the mound in Chicago during a game that Scott was pitching." After Scott shut out the Expos, Montreal pitcher Bryn Smith showed reporters balls that he said had been scuffed by Scott. "The guy cheats. There's no question about it," Smith declared.

In a classic case of the pot calling the kettle black, Kevin Gross publicly branded Scott a cheat. After pitching against Scott, Gross told reporters, "A few of the balls he used were still in the game in my half of the inning. So I used them, and I was amazed at some of the pitches I was able to throw. If I pitch in the same game as him, I'm just going to let him scuff the ball, and then I'll use it." Three weeks later, Gross was caught cheating and suspended. However, despite repeated spot checks by umpires of balls thrown by Scott, they have yet to find the hurler guilty of wrongdoing. "I suspect that Mike has quit doing it [scuffing the ball]," said the Houston source. "I've noticed that his ball doesn't have the erratic movement that it used to have. I think he stopped because he has so many batters thinking he throws scuffballs that it's just as effective as if he threw them."

As Scott's teammate Nolan Ryan toils in the twilight of a sparkling career, an increasing number of scuffball accusations have been fired at him. After Ryan beat the Braves in 1987, Atlanta manager Chuck Tanner produced 18 balls that he claimed had been doctored by Ryan. The year before, Reds pitcher Chris Welsh said every time he went to the mound and picked up the last ball Ryan used, "it was scuffed in the same spot—as if sandpaper had been rubbed across it."

Astros reliever Dave Smith has joined "the scuffball fraternity" too, claims Mets coach Bill Robinson. "I think I've seen Scott and Ryan doing things with the ball and I'm 100 percent sure that Smith does it. But we don't complain too much because we have success against him." Giants manager Roger Craig, who once coached both Scott and Smith, has vowed to catch Smith in the act. Craig, who convinced umpires to check balls thrown by Smith during a game with the Giants, declared, "I'll catch him scuffing one day because I know where he keeps the sandpaper."

Don Sutton, now of the Angels, has enjoyed his outlaw reputation ever since he was ejected in 1978 when umpires accused him of cheating. Sutton threatened to sue if he was suspended, so the league announced that he was not thumbed out for doctoring a baseball, but for throwing a doctored ball. "The only reason they caught Sutton was they found a skill saw hanging out of his back pocket," joked Steve Bedrosian of the Phillies. When the league didn't back the umpires, contends Madlock, "it meant pitchers didn't really have to worry about it [cheating]." Sutton has accepted his reputation for cutting balls with such good humor that he has even goaded umpires, says a teammate. "Once, an umpire went out to the mound to inspect his glove and the ump found a note that said, 'You're getting warm, but it's not here.' "

Sutton's pitching habits came under scrutiny in a 1987 game against the Orioles when acting manager Frank Robinson asked plate umpire Don Denkinger to confiscate several balls thrown by Sutton, which were forwarded to American League president Bobby Brown. "Sutton has scuffed balls for years," Robinson told the press. "I know because I used to be his teammate." No action was taken by the league.

Another moundsman players say has earned his "doctorate" is Rick Rhoden of the Yankees. During a 2–1 victory over the Orioles in 1987, Rhoden was confronted twice by umpires who discovered that balls he was throwing had been scuffed in precisely the same spot— across the words "American League." He was told that if one more doctored ball showed up, he was gone. None did. Twins manager Tom Kelly says he saves some of Rhoden's scuffballs. "I show them to friends and pass them around at the neighborhood bar," he said.

A ball allegedly doctored by Rhoden once so intrigued his pitching opponent, Don Carman of the Phillies, that Carman tried to use it—with disastrous results. "I was beating Rhoden 3–1 and they had a runner on third," recalls Carman. "The ump threw me a ball, and it had been scuffed up by Rhoden. So I thought I'd try it. I threw the ball and it jumped and got away from the catcher and cost me a run."

That doesn't happen to Tommy John of the Yankees. "If Tommy gets a ball with a scuff on it, he definitely knows what to do with it," claims Butch Wynegar, who sometimes caught for John in 1986. Claims a former Yankee teammate, "He's been doing it for years, but not all the time. It's only when he needs to."

The majority of major league pitchers don't cheat, many because they simply don't know how to use a scuffed ball. Says Wynegar, "I've told pitchers, 'I can get you a scuffed ball if you want it. And they've told me they wouldn't know what to do with it.' I was catching Willie Fraser [in a 1987 game] when he got a ball that was all scuffed up. It was perfect. He started the inning with it and he couldn't throw a strike because the ball was moving so much. Finally I went out and said, 'Willie, are you sure you want this ball?' And he shook his head, so we got another one from the ump."

▲

BROTHERLY LOVE

Just days after Joe Niekro was given a 10-day suspension for having an emery board and sandpaper in his hip pocket, his brother Phil was traded from the Indians to the Blue Jays. When he joined his new team, Phil discovered that some practical jokers had taped a note and two pieces of sandpaper above his locker. The note read: "Phil— thought you could use these during my 10-day vacation. Your brother, Joe."

▲

HOW DO PITCHERS DOCTOR THE BALL?

When it comes to cheating on the mound, today's pitchers specialize in scuffing or cutting the ball. "There are very few spitball pitchers now," says Phillies coach Claude Osteen. "Pitchers are into defacing the ball."

Those pitchers with the "right scuff" usually use sandpaper. "You can make it look like a routine scuff that the AstroTurf puts on the ball," says Osteen. "The only difference is that on doctored balls, the scuff mark is in the same place every time."

Mound doctors often glue sandpaper to the bottom of their glove. Before he was nabbed for cheating, Joe Niekro sometimes glued a piece of sandpaper to the palm of his glove hand, revealed Butch Wynegar of the Angels. "That way, when he rubbed up the ball, he'd scuff it up too."

Those who cut the ball rub it up against the sharpened eyelets of their glove, a belt buckle, or a thumbtack taped to a finger on the glove hand. A cut or scuffed ball is scraped on the wide section of the ball between the seams. The pitcher holds the ball with the cut side opposite where he wants the ball to break. For example, if the ball is thrown with the cut on the right, the ball will break left, or away from a righthanded hitter. By scuffing or cutting the ball on the top side just behind the horseshoe of the seam, a pitcher can make it drop by as much as half a foot. For a rising fastball, the pitcher throws the ball cut-side down.

Joe Sambito of the Red Sox says he's found a perfect way to throw a scuffed ball—without illegally scuffing it. "At times, I've intentionally thrown the ball in the dirt during warm-ups in hopes of getting it scuffed. If I get the scuff in the right spot and the umpire doesn't check it, then I've got a scuffed ball. I'm surprised more hitters don't ask the umpire to check the ball after it's been thrown in the dirt."

To load up a ball, pitchers use saliva, sweat, or petroleum jelly. When applied to the ball on the wide spot between the seams, the foreign substance takes away the spin and the ball drops as if rolled off a table. A little dab of K-Y jelly in an armpit, on a thigh, under the bill of the cap, or on the back of the neck—when mixed with a bit of sweat on the fingers—can give any hurler a major league sinker.

"When I was with the Giants, Jim Gott would keep the jelly right under his shoelaces," recalls Greg Minton of the Angels. "Whenever he needed some, he'd call time and tie his shoes. Give me a ball with some Vaseline and I can do some strange things with it. The Vaseline changes the rotation completely. It has a tumbling effect and makes the ball sink. My problem is I can't hit the broad side of a barn with it."

Few pitchers these days use sweat or saliva. The greasy kid stuff is on the way out too (even though grease balls of K-Y jelly "give you a great spitter," says Osteen). Pitchers are reluctant to throw a loaded ball because it's hard to master, requires a stiff wrist, and can hurt the arm. Not only that but a spitter has to be reloaded while a scuffed ball can be used again and again. Also, when playing on abrasive artificial surfaces, it's easy for the pitcher to claim that the ball was scuffed by the AstroTurf if he's challenged.

"It's fun to experiment," says Minton. "As long as hitters can cork their bats, we pitchers can monkey with the balls."

▲
TRUE CONFESSIONS

When Twins reliever George Frazier was with the Cubs, he boldly and repeatedly announced to the press before the 1985 season that a spitball was part of his pitching repertoire.

Where did all this braggadocio get him? Plenty of harassment from the umpires. "It was nice of George to tip us off," league administrator Blake Cullen said. "No matter who it is, Frazier or anyone else, it has to be stopped. It's my job and the job of the umpires to see that it is."

For the next two years, Frazier repeatedly was checked and examined by umpires and suffered the two worst seasons of an otherwise decent career. His ERA ballooned from a five-year average of 3.28 to a whopping 6.39 in 1985 and 5.06 in 1986.

▲
HOW DO PITCHERS GET BORDERLINE PITCHES CALLED STRIKES?

No matter how many pitches find the strike zone, they aren't strikes unless the umpire says they are. Since most effective pitchers nibble at the corners, it's vital that borderline pitches be called strikes. As a result, hurlers must do whatever they can to get close pitches called in their favor.

According to the *Baseball Confidential* survey, squawking at the umps seldom works. In fact, it usually backfires. However, some wily veterans have learned the art of subtle intimidation to sway umps just enough to turn balls into strikes.

"Nolan Ryan is great at intimidation," says teammate Charlie Kerfeld of the Astros. "He'll keep glaring at the ump on those close pitches until pretty soon the strike zone seems to get a little bit bigger." Another admiring Astro called Ryan's stare "an indescribable glower—it goes right through the ump. Ryan will use it early in every game, on the very first pitch if he has to. It's his way of changing the umpire to his way of thinking."

Tommy John of the Yankees has developed a cagey method of intimidating the home plate arbiter. "Tommy does it without saying a word," says the Tigers' Kirk Gibson. "I saw the way he works the umpire the last time we faced him. In the first inning, Tommy threw me a fastball that was low and just out of the strike zone for a ball. Tommy just kind of shook his head a little bit. The next pitch was in the same spot for another called ball and again he shook his head, not flagrantly, but just enough that the umpire could see it. The third pitch also was low but this time the ump called it a strike. I turned to the umpire and said, 'Hey, that goddamn ball is low. Don't take that shit from him. Don't look at him.' Throughout that whole game, Tommy set that umpire up to where Tommy was definitely getting the marginal pitches."

Some pitchers, especially the younger ones, try to badger the ump into calling strikes on borderline pitches. But experience shows that fiery tempers only inflame the situation. Says Mark Clear of the Brewers, "I used to yell at the ump things like, 'Where the fuck was that pitch!' But all that did was make him mad and he wouldn't give me the next close pitch. Since I stopped questioning balls and strikes, it seems like I'm getting more calls."

Clear's teammate, Paul Mirabella, learned the same lesson. "There are a lot of umpires who, if you show them up or continuously give them a hard time, will get the best of you in the long run. They'll retaliate by not giving you the close pitches." Most hurlers have discovered that the more a pitcher argues over balls and strikes during the course of the game, the smaller the strike zone becomes. "For example," said Mirabella, "in the 1985 World Series, Joaquin Andujar got hot-tempered with the home plate ump and the strike zone shrunk on him. Then he argued so much that he got ejected."

Sometimes bitching can't be helped, says Bryn Smith of the Expos. "I've had my run-ins with umps and hated them all. It's nothing personal. It's just that the adrenaline is flowing and you have a tendency to lose your cool every once in a while."

Kerfeld said he'll argue with some umpires, but not Frank Pulli. "Once he gets his Italian temper going, forget it. I try not to piss him off." Tom Candiotti of the Indians stays mum when Steve Palermo is behind the plate because "he gets the red ass real quick," said the hurler. "If you even look at him cross-eyed, his short fuse gets lit." An American League pitcher claims that John Shulock holds grudges against complaining hurlers. "If you question too many of his calls, I can guarantee you that you're not going to get anything close from him."

The hardest—but most effective—thing a pitcher can do is keep quiet on the mound after the ump has blown a call, said Dan Plesac of the Brewers. "When the ump makes a bad call, I tell myself, 'Get the ball back, get back to work, and forget about it.' I can't let that pitch affect the way I throw the next few pitches. It's hard to do, especially when it's a crucial point in a game and you lost the hitter on a 3–2 pitch."

Diplomacy definitely works on the mound. Steve Bedrosian of the Phillies is convinced that tight-lipped pitchers are more likely to get favorable calls. "I found out that if you keep your mouth shut on most of the calls, the umps have a tendency to give you the benefit of the doubt on a pitch that could go either way simply because you kept your cool."

The Royals' Bret Saberhagen says he never questions an umpire *during* the inning. "If I have a question, I might ask him after the inning is over. You don't want to show him up."

Pitchers such as Roger Clemens of the Red Sox aren't afraid to go up to the umpire right before the game and politely lay it on the line. "I'll go up to the ump and say, 'Listen, I'm working with you so work with me. Don't give me anything I don't deserve, but then again, don't take anything away from me. If the game gets down to the seventh inning and it's close, I can't afford to have you miss any pitches.' "

Mike Flanagan tries to soften home plate arbiters with a few kind words before the game—something his hotheaded former manager Earl Weaver never could do. "There's an umpire who's known for his hair-trigger temper and the first time you give him the wrong look, he's screaming at you," says Flanagan. "But I learned that if I went out of my way before I went to the mound and was pleasant to him, he'd call a good game." What words did the trick for Flanagan? Very simple ones: "Hi, how are you doing? Let's have a good game—and don't let Earl bother you."

PITCHERS WHO DON'T LOOK LIKE ATHLETES

1. Kent Tekulve
2. Charlie Kerfeld
3. Rick Reuschel
4. Oil Can Boyd
5. Jack Lazorko

HOW PITCHERS COPE WITH THE EVER-CHANGING STRIKE ZONE

Pitchers are the first to admit that not all umps have the same strike zone. Because the rules concerning balls and strikes are so ambiguous, some umpires have a smaller strike zone than others do.

A recent study confirmed what players already knew—there are hitters' umps and pitchers' umps. For example, American League batters coaxed 7.9 walks per game with Derryl Cousins behind the plate but only 5.36 walks with Jim McKean. In the senior circuit, Dick Stello called ball four an average of 7.98 times per game compared to 5.62 for Doug Harvey. The major league average is 6.66 walks per game.

Because of the disparity in the size of the strike zone from day to day, it's up to the pitcher to know whether the home plate umpire has a big or small strike zone. "The pitchers and umps are supposed to work together to put on a good ball game and it helps me to know where the strike zone is with that particular umpire," says Kent Tekulve of the Phillies. "I will ask him where a pitch was, trying to determine his strike zone. That way I know where I can or can't throw to get a strike."

It's sometimes easier said than done. "I must question the ump to establish the strike zone but some umps think I'm questioning their ability or trying to show them up," said an All-Star hurler. "That can be a problem. But we have a right to know whether he's calling them high or low."

Knowing the tendencies of the home plate umpire is so important to Roger Clemens of the Red Sox that he actually keeps a record on every arbiter. "I have cards on all the umpires, so once I learn who's going to be behind the plate when I pitch, I pull out the card and go over it. That way I know if he's a high-ball or low-ball ump or an inside or outside ump. There are also a lot of great umpires in the league who have a fair strike zone."

Clemens said that whenever he pitches with a new umpire behind the plate, he questions him just to get a mental picture of his strike zone. "For example, [in a 1987 game] I had a rookie ump named Jim Joyce. My first three innings were spent not only getting the batters out but also drawing information out from the umpire. I needed to know where his limits were so I could throw to a certain location and feel confident that I could get that crucial strikeout pitch."

Dan Plesac of the Brewers says pitchers can accept an ump who has a tighter strike zone just as long as he's consistent. "He's got to keep it from the first inning to the ninth so you know which pitches you're going to get and which ones you're not. It gets frustrating when an ump's strike zone changes from inning to inning because then you don't know where to throw the ball. Fortunately, I haven't seen a real bad ump yet. I think they all do a good job."

However, says Phillies pitching coach Claude Osteen, sometimes a pitcher dreads going out on the mound when a certain ump is behind the plate. "Some umps are worse at calling balls and strikes than others are. We all know who they are. The pitcher is usually resigned to the fact that the ump is going to miss lot of pitches. But he hopes that when he does miss them, they don't come at the wrong time.

There's another problem with inconsistency. When an ump realizes that he's missed a few, then he'll try to even things out and it ends up coming at the wrong time."

Umpires work hard to be consistent, adds Clemens. "But they have the same pressures that we do and they have their off nights just like we do. All I hope is that I don't catch one of them on an off night."

 ## WHO ARE THE BIGGEST SHOWBOATS ON THE MOUND?

1. **Oil Can Boyd**
2. **Dennis Eckersley**
3. **Joaquin Andujar**
4. **Juan Berenguer**
5. **Pascual Perez**

Nothing irks a batter more than being shown up by a pitcher.

"There's an unwritten rule that you don't show up pitchers and they don't show up batters," says Butch Wynegar. "Sometimes pitchers break that rule."

Chief offender is Oil Can Boyd of the Red Sox. "He struts and parades around the mound every time he gets me out—which is regularly," says Tom Brunansky of the Twins. Lenn Sakata of the Yankees adds, "He punches the air when he strikes you out."

"The Can" has received so much heat—even Reggie Jackson ripped Boyd for showing up the opposition—that he told the press he felt intimidated. "I haven't pitched well since I started listening to the guys tell me I'm showing them up," he lamented. "I'm not a hotdog. I just want to have fun. I create my own atmosphere, and when I don't have that atmosphere around me, I'm not the same pitcher."

The enmity directed at Dennis Eckersley of the Athletics spans both leagues. "When he pitched for the Cubs, everybody on our team really got pumped up because of the stuff he did on the mound," said Wallace Johnson of the Expos. "He acts like he's Cy Young out there." Adds the Twins' Kirby Puckett, "Eckersley will form his fingers into a gun and then shoot you down after you strike out." When he's hot and gets two strikes on a batter, Eckersley has been known to yell at the man on deck, "You're next!"

Eckersley's teammate Joaquin Andujar is another hurler who loves to shoot down strike-out victims with an imaginary gun. "If he gets two strikes on you, he tries to embarrass you," claims Jim Gantner of the Brewers. "I try to see that he doesn't get two strikes on me." Gantner won't ever forget the way Andujar "gunned him down" during the 1982 World Series when Joaquin pitched for the Cardinals. "I hit the ball back to Andujar and he held the ball as long as he could before throwing it to first. When I ran by him, he went 'pow' and shot me with his fingers and said, 'I got ya.' I called him a hotdog and he went berserk. He wanted to fight right there and then but the ump broke it up. The guy is a hotdog."

A teammate admits that Twins reliever Juan Berenguer gets so pumped up at times that he forgets what he's doing. During the second game of the 1987 American League Championship Series, while striking out the side in the ninth inning to preserve a Twins victory, Juan repeatedly turned toward the Tigers' dugout, shouted at them, and thrust his fist in the air. An annoyed Sparky Anderson, manager of the Tigers, said, "When you've got a sleeping dog down, you don't kick him or try to embarrass him. When the dog wakes up, he sometimes bites you."

Pascual Perez of the Expos struts so much on the mound after getting out a tough batter that "he ought to be a drum major," says a Cub. Adds a Met, "There's not enough mustard to cover Perez. He's such a hotdog."

▲

HARD TO TELL

After the Padres' first three batters—Marvell Wynne, Tony Gwynn, and John Kruk—all belted successive first-inning homers off Roger Mason of the Giants in an early-season game in 1987, San Francisco manager Roger Craig went out to the mound. He turned to catcher Bob Melvin and said, "Does he have good stuff?" Replied Melvin, "I don't know. I haven't caught any pitches yet."

THE
BULLPEN

WHAT REALLY GOES ON IN THE BULLPEN?

Don't think for a moment that the bullpen crew spends all its time concentrating on the game. Far removed from their team and the on-field action, these relievers must kill more time than rallies. They fight boredom by focusing less on the game than on amusing themselves.

"You need a diversion because you can get so tight waiting to be called in a crucial, late-inning situation that you could go nuts," says reliever Paul Assenmacher of the Braves. Adds Greg Minton of the Angels, "It doesn't hurt to have a devil-may-care attitude in the bullpen because you can turn from a hero to a goat very quickly when you come in with the game on the line. If you're not crazy when you first go out to the bullpen, you will be soon enough."

To pass the time and ease the pressure, relievers conduct everything from "scientific experiments" to crazy contests in the bullpen—usually out of sight of the manager in the dugout. Says Bill Madlock of the Tigers, "I've been around a long time and I think relievers generally have so much fun in the bullpen that half of them don't want to get into the game."

The location of the bullpen can determine how much a player gets away with. Pens in foul territory like those in Houston's Astrodome, situated only a few steps outside the dugout, tend to put a damper on tomfoolery. On the other hand, those pens tucked away beyond the outfield fence and out of sight of the dugout allow for greater freedom.

Relievers who enjoy pastoral pursuits often compile lists for such things as an All-Ugly Team, an All-Skinny Team, or an All-Slob Team. Spitting contests, which call for distance and accuracy, have always been big. Bullpen denizens often play games such as "Password" or "Name That Tune." However, admits Dan Quisenberry of the Royals, "Most of us can't carry a tune, so it's real difficult to give the correct answer." The Quiz once organized a daily attendance-guessing contest in the bullpen which he won with uncommon regularity—until his teammates discovered his secret. "I used to call the ticket office every night and find out how many tickets were sold," he confessed. "It was pretty hard to lose that way until I got caught."

Groundskeepers often provide relief pitchers with a diversion. "We'll talk to them," says Quisenberry. "They have lots of stuff for us to play with like tools and rakes. You can take off a handle and practice your golf swing." The Royals' relievers like the grounds-keepers so much that they leave them money. "On the last day of the home stand, the relievers hide 20 dollars somewhere in the bullpen and the grounds crew goes and looks for it," says Buddy Black. "If they don't find it, then it increases to 40 dollars at the end of the next home stand and it keeps going up until someone finds it."

In Atlanta, the Braves relievers often play checkers with the groundskeepers, whose room is right outside the bullpen door. The groundskeepers have helped hurlers Gene Garber and Jim Acker tend a flower garden in the bullpen. "We spend two or three hours a day down there, so we might as well make the surroundings nice," says teammate Paul Assenmacher. "They spend a few hours before the game planting and pruning flowers and they panic when one of the plants isn't doing so well. They take it seriously." So do members of the Royals relief corps, who have been engaged in a tomato-growing contest in the bullpen.

Among the most enjoyable pastimes are the simplest—eating and sleeping. "Some guys have been known to take a little snooze," admits Kent Tekulve of the Phillies. "We all have roles and we know which part of the game we might have to pitch in and which we don't. When it gets to the part where you're not going to pitch, the easiest thing to do is take a nap." Jerry Reed of the Mariners says some of the best sleep he's ever had has been in the bullpen. "I've fallen asleep for a few minutes and awakened fully refreshed." In 1984, nearly the entire Expos bullpen took turns napping, recalls Gary Lucas, now with the Angels. "We played a night game that went into extra innings and we didn't leave the ballpark until three A.M. Then we had to be back the next afternoon for a game. We were all tired so we decided to catch some winks. We took shifts."

Despite all the shenanigans, relievers still spend much of their time in the bullpen talking baseball. "It's really Baseball 101 down there," says Assenmacher. "We're always talking about how to pitch to certain guys. However, there are times when one minute you're talking baseball and the next you're discussing Robert E. Lee. There's never a dull moment."

When Terry Forster was with the Angels in 1986, he could never sit out in the bullpen for more than ten minutes without saying something profound, says Lucas. "During one game, Terry turned to [bullpen coach] Bob Clear and said, 'Bobaloo, Bobaloo, I know you're watching the game, but I gotta ask you something. Would you rather pitch in the seventh game of the World Series or have a sure-thing date with Victoria Principal?' And Bob told him. 'What the fuck does Victoria Principal have to do with the ballgame?' That's the bullpen for you."

SAYING A MOUTHFUL

The bullpen has always been known as a place where flakes get their reputations.

Take, for instance, Pirates pitcher Bob Walk, who has toiled as a reliever as well as a starter. "One day I was out in the bullpen when I caught a moth and stuck it in my mouth. I went up to one of the coaches and started talking to him and the moth flew out. Naturally, everyone started calling me a flake after that."

HOW SOME RELIEF PITCHERS PASS THE TIME IN THE BULLPEN

Dan Quisenberry, Royals: "I like to conduct insect experiments such as the tobacco test. The other night, we caught a yellow bug and then spit tobacco juice on it. Yellow bugs do not like tobacco juice—it's now a scientific fact."

Dave Stewart, Athletics: "I helped develop something called 'Master Pain.' It was started when I was with the Dodgers. It's to see who can stand the most pain. You sit there and pull hairs out of each other's nose. Is that wacky enough for you?"

DeWayne Buice, Angels: "During a game once, we made a replica of the stadium with dirt, grass, and things we found lying around in the bullpen. The light standards were made out of matchbooks and soda straws and the stands were made out of cardboard.

In the ninth inning, we lit all the matchbooks so our little field was well lighted."

Larry Andersen, Astros—He has mastered acupuncture—seed acupuncture. "Lots of players eat sunflower seeds," says teammate Charlie Kerfeld. "Well, if you open up the middle of a sunflower seed partway, you can attach it to your skin because it pinches. Larry loves to stick them all over his face. He calls it seed acupuncture. He'll make a mustache or an extra eyebrow out of sunflower seeds."

Joe Sambito, Red Sox: "We do some crazy things like hold beachball races. Fans will throw beachballs down to us and we'll gather up five or six of them. Then we use a marker to put a number on each one and line them up on the bullpen pitchers' mounds. Each guy has a numbered beachball and we wait for the wind to take them. The guy whose ball gets blown to the other side of the bullpen first wins."

Kent Tekulve, Phillies: "When the ballgame is a blowout, we've been known to play miniature golf in our bullpen. We'll dig some holes in the dirt and set up a little course where you have to go around the pitching mound to get to the hole. We use a baseball for a golf ball and a bat for a golf club."

Phillies' bullpen crew: "We like to catch bugs and use them as targets for spitting tobacco juice on them," says catcher Darren Daulton. "We try and drown them." He and his bullpen buddies also catch big black flies and turn them into airplane pilots. "We'll make a tiny paper airplane, glue the fly's feet to it, and watch him fly. Or we will capture a beetle, tie a string to it, and attach it to a little buggy made of matchsticks." Entomology aside, some relievers dabble in rocketry. "First, you collect matches and foil wrappers," says Phillies coach Claude Osteen. "You wrap the foil around the matchstick to build a miniature rocket. Then you launch it at the outfielders."

Scott Bailes, Indians: "One of the most popular bullpen pastimes throughout the league is sunflower-seed flipping. Everyone flips them. Rich Yett and I have contests to see who can flip sunflower seeds the farthest."

Dave Righetti, Yankees—He constantly needles his bullpen mates. "I stopped sitting near him," said one of his fellow relievers. "He rags on you mercilessly. That's how he kills time."

CAUGHT IN THE ACT

To pass the time during a boring game at Comiskey Park in Chicago in 1984, Brewer relievers Pete Ladd and Tom Tellmann were playing bocci ball, or lawn bowling, in the bullpen.

The two were rolling baseballs on the ground, figuring they were too far out of sight of the manager to get into any trouble. All of a sudden, they looked up at the scoreboard. To their chagrin and surprise, Ladd and Tellmann discovered that their bocci-ball game was being televised on DiamondVision for everybody in the ball park to see—including Brewers general manager Harry Dalton, who later reprimanded them.

SNEAKING A SNACK IN THE BULLPEN

One of the best perks about spending the season in the bullpen is sneak eating. Pitchers chow down out there all the time—and not just a simple snack like a hotdog or a candy bar. We're talking plates of ribs and whole pizzas.

"There are a few players who might consider consuming a few edible items in the bullpen," said Kent Tekulve with a grin. "Actually, there are more than just a few."

Jerry Royster of the White Sox said he has been on teams where pizzas were ordered out to the bullpen—and delivered. "When I was with the Braves, we would place an order before batting practice and the pizza guy would go to the stadium, through the stands, and into the back entrance of the bullpen. By the time the game started, the pizza would be waiting for us. Best of all, we never got caught."

Typically, relievers have a supplier whose job is to sneak goodies from the clubhouse to the bullpen. On the Angels, for example, it's rookie DeWayne Buice. "Since he's the low man on the totem pole in terms of major league service, he has to bring the towels with him down to the bullpen," says veteran Gary Lucas. "You can get a lot of things hidden between those towels. DeWayne does a good job on this club. I call him 'Snacks' because he's always got some snacks for us. Whatever is available in the clubhouse finds it way to the bullpen so we don't go hungry."

The most common approach for obtaining food in the bullpen is enlisting the aid of a fan. "We're not allowed to eat in the bullpen, but we eat there all the time," says Phillies top reliever Steve Bedrosian. "We do what most guys do—we trade balls for food like a Coke and a bag of peanuts. When I was with Atlanta, we had fans buy us ice cream in exchange for a ball. But we got caught and fined."

The Yankees bullpen crew has actually auctioned balls off to fans before the game, says the Angels' Butch Wynegar, a former Yankee. "Some players stuff the pockets of their warm-up jackets with baseballs and go out there before the game to auction them off. The fans with the highest bid then buy hotdogs and drinks and give them to the players before getting their baseballs. And people have wondered why those guys gained weight during the season."

Ron Davis was responsible for one of the more memorable sneak-eating binges in the Yankee bullpen, recalls former teammate Paul Mirabella, now of the Brewers. "He ate four Burger King fish sandwiches two minutes before he went into the game. He had given a fan a ball to get them for him."

Charlie Kerfeld, the Astros' 6-foot, 6-inch, 230-pound, full-time eating machine and part-time reliever, says he maintains his figure by swapping balls for hotdogs and pizza. Two weeks after returning from a stint in the minors in 1987, Kerfeld somehow got two huge plates of barbequed ribs during a game at Shea Stadium. He was contentedly munching away in the bullpen out of sight of the dugout—but not out of the range of the TV cameras. The ribs cost him a $250 fine.

HOW DO BULLPEN PITCHERS
SPELL RELIEF? F-A-N-S

Bullpen pitchers have cultivated some bizarre relationships with fans to while away the time.

"I'm looking to be entertained when I'm in the bullpen," says Dan Quisenberry of the Royals. "Fans often provide it. Many of the same fans sit near our bullpen night after night. We know all their faces and have nicknames for them. One guy looks like a cross between the Kentucky Fried Chicken colonel and Santa Claus. Then there's a guy who always wears army fatigues so we call him Phnom Penh."

During the dog days of summer, Quisenberry himself sometimes grabs the fire hose in the right-field bullpen and sprays the fans in the general admission seats during the seventh-inning stretch to cool them off.

Bullpen pitchers get heated up by scanning the stands for sexy women, admits Dan Plesac of the Brewers. "A lot of girl-watching goes on out there because there's plenty of nice scenery in the seats. If you sit out there for 162 games and watch every pitch, you get bored after a while. The guys have to do something to break up the monotony."

One surveyed pitcher says he and his bullpen teammates go well beyond just eyeballing pretty fans. "We talk to them all the time— even get dates that way."

The Reds bullpen flips sunflower seeds at the sexiest fans, says Cincinnati's Tom Browning. "[Reds reliever] Rob Murphy doesn't just shoot sunflower seeds anywhere into the stands. He shoots at targets. He tries to hit girls' tits."

Friendly female fans make sitting in the bullpen worthwhile, says Angels relief ace Donnie Moore. "I was in the bullpen once when a lady flashed us. One of my teammates responded by mooning her. So she flashed us again and he mooned her again. But I'll never tell who he was."

Teammate Greg Minton says one of the greatest challenges facing a relief pitcher today is talking a pretty fan into giving him her bra or panties. "Sometimes it takes a whole three-game series before you can get them. A monumental highlight on a personal level can be trading a ball for a girl's panties."

Such collector's items make terrific clubhouse trophies. Recalls Bill Dawley of the Cardinals, "When I played for Houston in 1985, we managed to get a fan to toss us her bra in exchange for a baseball during a game in Pittsburgh. We kept it in the locker room and used it as a gag gift. If a pitcher on our team went out and got his tits lit [was shelled on the mound], then he got the bra. He kept it in his locker until someone else got their tits lit."

BULLPEN: ENTER AT YOUR OWN RISK

Roger Clemens of the Red Sox discovered the hard way that starting pitchers don't belong in the bullpen.

Between starts early in the 1987 season, Clemens decided to watch a game from the bullpen instead of the dugout where starters normally stay. "I was told that you've got to be prepared for anything if you go down there," Clemens recalled. "I wasn't there five minutes when one of the guys in the bullpen shouted, 'Oh, look, look! There's a fight breaking out in the stands!' I got up from my seat, turned around, and the next thing I knew, everyone in the bullpen started punching me. Those guys are a tough bunch."

PHONEY BUSINESS

During almost every game, the manager or his pitching coach calls the bullpen to give instructions on who should warm up or sit down. But sometimes communications get botched.

In 1985, Jerry Koosman of the Phillies nearly didn't finish his first shutout victory of the year because of a breakdown in communications. Don Carman was warming up in the bullpen when Phils pitching coach Claude Osteen got on the dugout telephone before the start of the eighth inning. "I called down to the bullpen and [catcher] Ozzie Virgil answered," recalled Osteen. "I told Ozzie to sit Carman down. He thought I said to send Carman in." Carman arrived on the mound to start the eighth inning. But before Carman threw a warm-up pitch, Koosman started yelling from the dugout. "Fortunately, we got Carman off the mound in time," said Osteen. "If he had thrown a warm-up pitch, he would have had to stay in. After that, Virgil promised not to answer any more phones in the bullpen."

Don't knock White Sox bullpen coach Art Kusnyer if he's a little leery about answering the phone. "We decided to put shaving cream on the receiver of his bullpen phone as a prank during the last game of 1985," recalls reliever Gene Nelson, now of the Athletics. "We had planned to have [reserve catcher] Marc Hill call from the dugout during the third inning. What we didn't expect was that [Sox starting pitcher] Tom Seaver would give up too many runs in the first inning, causing [Sox manager] Tony LaRussa to call the bullpen. We tried to reach the phone first and clean up the mess but we were too late. Kusnyer picked up the phone and didn't notice the shaving cream. He couldn't hear LaRussa, so he shoved the phone harder into his ear. We were panicky that he would get mad at us but he laughed instead."

Of all the bullpen phone conversations overheard by Dan Quisenberry, none is more memorable than the one between Royals manager Dick Howser and coach Jim Schaffer in 1983. "Howser called down and told Schaffer to warm up Mike Armstrong and Bill Castro," the Quiz recalled. "A few minutes later, Schaffer called Howser and said, 'They're both ready.' Howser asked, 'Which one looks better?' And Schaffer replied, 'They're both ugly.' "

▲

NOW THAT'S REASSURING

In his first day in the major leagues in 1986, Indians relief pitcher Scott Bailes was hoping to hear some words of reassurance from veteran reliever Jamie Easterly while the two sat in the bullpen.

"I thought to myself, 'Man, I'm going to get nervous when that phone rings,' " Bailes recalled. "So I turned to Jamie and said, 'Do you get nervous when you hear the phone ring?' And he said, 'Naw, I've heard it a thousand times.' Then he looked me in the eye and said, 'No matter how many years you play, you can bet the first time you hear it ring in the new season, you have to check your pants.' "

THE
CLUB-
HOUSE

WHAT KINDS OF PRACTICAL JOKES DO PLAYERS PULL ON EACH OTHER IN THE CLUBHOUSE?

There are times when you step into a major league clubhouse and swear that you've entered Pee Wee Herman's playhouse. All around you pranksters are whooping and hollering, spraying shaving cream, cutting up someone's new clothes, hiding live snakes. Except these aren't kids. They are major league baseball players.

"You need a loosy-goosy kind of feeling," says Bill Scherrer of the Reds. "You want teammates laughing because the game is so serious—there's so much on the line. If a clubhouse is too tense and no one is talking, that's bad."

Usually jokesters pull their pranks on rookies, nice guys, and those players who can't take a joke. Recalls Frank DiPino of the Cubs, "Sarge [Gary Matthews] was the best target because everybody liked him. He never knew what was going to happen. One time they pulled the pegs out of his chair, and when he sat down, the chair collapsed."

Woe to the player whose secret fear is known by the rest of the team. For example, Joaquin Andujar of the Athletics is deathly afraid of snakes. "At Houston, they put a fake snake in his locker for two or three days straight," said a former teammate. "Andujar would get scared every time. On the fourth day, he walked into the clubhouse and said, 'I suppose you put another rubber snake in my locker. Well, I'm not going to fall for it again.' He reached in and pulled out a black snake—only this one was real and alive. He went nuts. He was such a wreck that he couldn't pitch that day—and he was supposed to start."

It's almost standard practice to target a player who has committed a blunder on the field. "We are all vulnerable during the season to do something stupid," says Dan Quisenberry of the Royals. "It can get tense, so you need to have someone break the mood with a practical joke."

The Phillies decided to poke a little fun at pitcher John Denny and his quick temper. "He flipped out after one game and got totally, unbelievably mad and tore up our clubhouse," recalls Kevin Gross. "The next day, some of the guys taped foam rubber all around his locker so he wouldn't get hurt—sort of like a padded cell. When he came in, he didn't think it was funny at all. But the rest of us did."

Batting slumps are sure to inspire pranksters. Angels center fielder Gary Pettis, who struggled at the plate throughout the 1987 season, was the victim of some clubhouse comedy. While Pettis was taking a nap, a teammate draped a towel over him as if he were a corpse, and placed a cardboard tombstone on his bat saying, "Gary Pettis, 1958–1987." During a 1986 road trip, when Vince Coleman of the Cardinals was mired in a 0-for-26 slump, a clubhouse jokester taped several of Coleman's bats together with a message that said, "Ship to St. Louis. Not needed."

The day after he was nicked for the game-winning hit in a 3-2 loss to the Mets in 1986, Phillies reliever Steve Bedrosian entered the clubhouse and found his locker empty. All his equipment had been removed. Pasted over his number on the stall was the name "Rhoden," after Rick Rhoden, whom the Phillies were trying to acquire from the Pirates. A steaming-mad Bedrosian recovered his equipment in the hallway outside the clubhouse.

Nothing beats messing with a players' clothes for sheer fun—unless, of course, they're your clothes. Glenn Hubbard of the Braves was "nailed" in a common clubhouse caper. "They nailed all my gloves, spikes, and clothes to my locker with two-inch nails," he said. "It took me about an hour to pry everything loose. Actually, that was a payback to the wrong person. They paid me back for something I didn't do."

"During a game once, [teammate] Bert Blyleven came into the clubhouse between innings and cut holes in my underwear and also shredded them," recalls Steve Lombardozzi of the Twins. Lombardozzi paid him back on the last day of the season by using one of George Brett's favorite tricks—cutting off the toes of a player's dress socks. "George did that to me once," says teammate Bret Saberhagen. "When I went to put on my socks, I had no toes and pulled them straight up to my knees. I could have used them on my arms as wristbands." Rather than cut up the polka-dotted underwear of Cardinals pitcher Joe Magrane, a jokester played connect the dots with a magic marker.

Here's the favorite prank of a Yankee who refuses to be named because he plans to use it on a teammate: "You take a guy's pants from his locker, get monofilament and thread it through the pants pocket down to his knee, and attach a banana peel to it. When he puts on his pants, he'll jump all over the room."

DeWayne Buice of the Angels says that in 1987 a teammate took 12 packs of Saltine crackers, crushed them, stuck them in the shoes of pitcher John Candelaria, and got them wet. "Candelaria thought that George Hendrick did it but he didn't," said Buice. "The real culprit then decided to pull a trick on Hendrick to make him think that Candelaria did it. So the guy got a can [of a sticky substance] and sprayed it all over George's shower shoes. When George put them on, they stuck to the soles of his feet and he couldn't get them off. George shouted out, 'That damn Candy Man put Superglue in my shoes!' " (The real culprit turned out to be teammate Jack Fimple.)

Many practical jokes are pulled off when the targeted player is showering or napping. "Mitch Williams [of the Rangers] is always in a hurry to take a shower and rush out," says manager Bobby Valentine. "So a few times, the guys have taken his clothes and hid them while he's in the shower." Reid Nichols of the Expos has mastered the shaving-cream-in-the-towel trick, says Montreal beat writer Wesley Goldstein. "He's done it to at least a half-dozen players in 1987. Once the players are in the shower, Reid takes their white towels and sprays one side full of shaving cream. When they come out, with their eyes half closed, they grab their towel, wipe themselves, and end up with shaving cream all over them."

When Bill Madlock joined the Tigers in midseason in 1987, he quickly discovered the dangers of a pregame nap in the clubhouse. Says teammate Kirk Gibson, "Alan Trammell and Mike Heath—who have done this to Bill a couple of times—wait until he's all nice asleep and then they sprinkle baby powder all over him. When he wakes up, he sees he's white."

Every year on every team, it seems someone falls victim to the fake-trade scam. On the Cubs in 1987, it was star hurler Rick Sutcliffe, who the year before limped into the clubhouse with his leg in a fake cast, causing waves of panic in the front office. So Cubs president Dallas Green decided to get even. He left a message on Sutcliffe's locker saying that the pitcher had been traded to Pittsburgh. Sutcliffe was stunned. He walked into Green's office, which was crowded with somber-faced team officials, and asked, "Who am

I being traded for?" Before Green could answer, everyone burst out laughing.

But players generally agree that the best trade prank in recent years was pulled off in 1986 by the Angels' Jerry Reuss when he was with the Dodgers. Reuss, the subject of trade rumors the previous winter, played his trick when the Dodgers were in Chicago for an early-season game with the Cubs at the same time the Yankees were playing the White Sox across town. With equipment bag in hand, Reuss reported for duty in the Yankees clubhouse at Comiskey Park. He walked into manager Lou Piniella's office and said, "Here I am. I'm your new pitcher and I'll do whatever you want, start or relieve." Piniella was shocked. "What are you talking about?" he demanded. Reuss replied, "Didn't George call you?" When Piniella said he'd had no word from Yankees owner George Steinbrenner, Reuss suggested, "Then we'd better close the door and talk." Only then did Reuss reveal the joke, which Piniella took with good humor. Said Reuss proudly, "It probably was my best prank."

GETTING CREAMED

The Cubs decided to do something special to mark the 40th birthday of assistant trainer Dick Cummings in 1987.

"Some of the players trapped him in the training room and pinned him down on the table," recalls Chicago beat writer Fred Mitchell. "Then Ryne Sandberg, Rick Sutcliffe, and Keith Moreland wrapped elastic tape around Cummings' body to keep him down. Next, they sprayed shaving cream all over his body and stuck something resembling a big candle in the middle of it all. Then they sang 'Happy Birthday.' "

WHAT PRACTICAL JOKES DO ROOKIES FALL FOR EVERY YEAR?

1. The Three-Man Lift
2. The Ugly Shoe Swap
3. The Wild Mongoose Prank
4. The Cake Slam

Many veterans love to give a big—and unforgettable—welcome to rookies by setting them up.

For instance, when Angels pitcher Jerry Reuss was with the Dodgers in 1984, he decided to have a little fun during spring training at the expense of the rookies. Swiping some stationery from the Dodgertown infirmary, Reuss, using a doctor's name, wrote letters to eight rookies telling them that something was wrong with the blood samples taken during their spring-training physicals. They were told to bring a sperm sample to the nurse first thing in the morning. Sure enough, four rookies sheepishly showed up at the infirmary carrying their samples in motel glasses.

It's unlikely that Reuss's great stunt could ever be repeated so successfully. However, year in and year out, the following four practical jokes are pulled on rookies in almost every clubhouse—and they always work:

The Three-Man Lift

Pete Incaviglia of the Rangers gained firsthand knowledge about the three-man lift after making the team in 1986. "I was in the clubhouse when [teammates] Larry Parrish, Toby Harrah, and Bobby Jones were talking about how Jones could lift three people at once. I said, 'No way, you're crazy.' So Toby said, 'I bet you Bobby can pick up you, Joe, and Larry.' So I made the bet. They told me to lay on the floor between Parrish and Ferguson and interlock my arms and legs with theirs, which I did. Bobby flexed his muscles and took a few deep breaths and then suddenly he ripped my shirt open and pulled down my pants. I couldn't move because my arms and legs were locked. Then everyone in the clubhouse ran over and poured cologne, mustard, shaving cream, stuff from spittoon boxes, and everything you can imagine all over me. I was covered from head to toe. I don't think I ever laughed so hard in my life. I fell right into that one."

The Ugly Shoe Swap

Rookies face being victimized by the ugly shoe swap whenever their team travels to Atlanta. "It's an annual thing in the Giants organization," says former Giant Rob Deer, now with the Brewers. "They got me when I was a rookie. In Atlanta, there's a shoe store where you can get shoes for 50 cents a pair. They are the ugliest shoes you've ever seen—like bright canary-yellow patent leathers with heels three inches high and zippers down the side and checkerboards on the front. The veterans bought about a dozen of them and then, on getaway day, they stole all the rookies' shoes out of their lockers and replaced them with these ugly shoes. The rookies would have to wear them on the plane and in the hotel and wouldn't get their good shoes back until the next day. I still have my pair."

The Wild Mongoose Prank

National League rookies need to worry not only about Atlanta but about Cincinnati as well. Clubhouse man Roger Wilson has a big wooden box with a steel grating and a sign that says, DANGER: WILD MONGOOSE. Ed Lynch of the Cubs describes how it's used: "Someone will start talking about Roger's wild mongoose and how dangerous it is and go into a very elaborate story that makes the rookie want to see it. So the rookie gets real close to the grating and all he sees is a tail, which is really a large, bushy raccoon tail attached to a spring and trip wire. Roger will stand there and kind of poke the tail and it jumps around giving the impression that the 'animal' is alive. Then when the rookie gets real close, Roger trips the wire and this raccoon tail flies out of the box right at the rookie. You see some of the funniest reactions. We've had guys climb lockers. We got Shawon Dunston and Chico Walker [both of the Cubs] so good they ran all the way across the clubhouse."

The Cake Slam

There's an even simpler practical joke that gets 'em every time— the cake slam. One of its victims in 1987 was Bo Jackson of the

Royals. "They brought in a birthday cake and the guys were going around saying the cake smelled funny," recalls teammate Kevin Seitzer. "So Bo came along and bent over to sniff it. Just then Sabes [Bret Saberhagen] pushed Bo's face right into the cake."

Saberhagen was introduced to the world of major league practical jokes during spring training of his rookie year in 1984. "About ten of us went out to a Mexican restaurant and started drinking tequila," Saberhagen remembers. "They kept ordering tequila and I kept up with them round after round. Then we started drinking double shots. Finally, I stood up to leave and I got sick all over the back of the table. Not until the next day did I find out that they had worked something out with the waitress. Whenever they ordered a round, she brought me a shot of tequila and brought them a shot of water."

▲

ODD BALLS

When rookies on the Giants arrive in Chicago for the first time, they must carry out a bizarre team ritual.

"On the way to the ball park," says a Giant, "the team bus passes a statue of General Sheridan on a horse. At some point before we leave town, the rookies have to go out in the middle of the night and paint the horse's balls orange—which is one of the Giants' colors. When the deed is done and the team bus drives by the statue, all the veterans cheer. It's been going on for years."

▲

HOT-FOOTING IT AROUND THE LEAGUE

At one time or another almost every player has been hot-footed—the surreptitious lighting of shoelaces.

"The best I've ever seen is Ryne Sandberg," says Cubs teammate Keith Moreland. "Ryne has accomplices who talk to the victim and get his attention away from his feet. Then Ryne sneaks up behind him and lights his shoestrings. It sure scares them when they see their laces on fire."

But Sandberg, who admits hot-footing someone "about once a day," says he has developed a more effective technique. "I dab a little alcohol on the back of someone's foot and then light it. Alcohol burns quickly and it's hard to put out, so it's good to use."

Glenn Hubbard of the Braves will go to any lengths to hot-foot a victim, says former teammate Jerry Royster of the White Sox. "He'll slither like a snake under tables to light up someone's laces. He can even get someone who is sitting in the middle of the dugout bench. Glenn gets a coat hanger and straightens it out and puts bubble gum on the end of it. Then he sticks a match in the bubble gum, lights it, and shoves it next to the guy's shoelaces. He's been doing that for years."

The Mets' expert hot-footer, Roger McDowell, has kept his team hopping since his rookie year in 1985. "Every two minutes you have to check the back of your shoes because they might be on fire thanks to Roger," says coach Bill Robinson. "He got me during a game in 1986. I was walking out to the coach's box when all of a sudden I felt something hot shooting up the back of my leg. I turned around, looked down, and saw that the heel of my shoe was on fire. There were 20,000 fans at Shea Stadium all looking at me and laughing. Now that's embarrassing. I wanted to kill him."

Dwayne Murphy of the Athletics says the best hot-foot he ever pulled victimized teammate Mike Norris. "I went up to [teammate] Tony Armas and said, 'Mike wants to get you real bad so I'll tell you what we'll do. You put on his baseball shoes without him knowing it and then sit in the lounge. I'll give him a lighter and tell him where you are.' Armas agreed and put on Norris's shoes. I went over to Norris, gave him the lighter, and whispered, 'Mike, there's Tony. Go get him.' So Norris crawled military style across the floor under the table and finally lit the shoelaces. Then he jumped up and shouted, 'I got you! I got you!' After the shoe all but burned up, Armas called Norris over and said, 'Look at this.' Then he pulled back the tongue of the shoe and Norris saw that it was his number."

WHAT STRANGE THINGS DO PLAYERS KEEP IN THEIR LOCKERS?

Like kids stashing all sorts of neat items in their bottom dresser drawer, ballplayers store some of the weirdest things you can imagine in their lockers—from lizard tails to ugly naked dolls to handcuffs.

Here's a sampling around the majors of the weird and wacky things that players keep in their lockers:

Kent Tekulve, Phillies: "Kent keeps a hairy, naked, ugly, gross doll in his locker," says teammate Kevin Gross. It was given to Tekulve by a fan, and for some reason, he has taken a shine to it. Now it stays in his locker at Veterans Stadium. "It's real grotesque to look at and the more we try to make him get rid of it, the more adamant he is that it stays," says Philadelphia beat writer Bill Brown.

Frank DiPino, Cubs: "He has a gray hat with fake shit on it that he keeps in his locker," said a teammate. "It's a hat for a shit head."

Ron Kittle, Yankees: "I've had bras and garters autographed by fans that I kept in my locker—when I was single."

Bill Caudill, Athletics: "When he was with Seattle, he was nicknamed 'Inspector' because he kept an Inspector Clouseau hat and handcuffs in his locker," says a teammate. "He would chain guys up too."

Mickey Hatcher, Dodgers—He keeps a picture of his hero, idol, and role model—Rodney Dangerfield—in his locker.

Gene Garber, Braves: "He chews so much tobacco and spits it all over the place that they got him a gold spittoon for his locker," says former teammate Jerry Royster.

Marty Barrett, Red Sox—He stores a good-luck crystal in his locker. After he brought it to the clubhouse in 1986, the Red Sox won 15 of 18 games, including 11 in a row.

Gary Gaetti, Twins: "He has a rubber ball in his locker and it has an ugly face with big eyes and a tongue hanging out," says teammate Steve Lombardozzi.

Von Hayes, Phillies—A stuffed wild goose with a couple of Phillies sweat bands sits on top of his locker. He killed it during the off-season.

Goose Gossage, Padres: "The goose has some kind of animal with antlers wearing sunglasses and a hat that's on top of his locker," says teammate Tony Gwynn.

Ozzie Guillen, White Sox: "I keep a lizard tail in my locker because my daddy gave it to me and told me that it would bring good luck."

Nolan Ryan, Astros—For the last three years, Ryan has kept a large poster of bulky teammate Charlie Kerfeld in his locker.

Mark McElmore, Angels: "He has a picture of Janet Jackson," says teammate DeWayne Buice. "He's in love with her. He gets upset when you talk bad about her."

▲

AND THE WINNER IS . . .

To keep things loose in the clubhouse, teams often present a special off-the-wall award either to the player who was the game's MVP or to the guy who screwed up the most. Here's a sampling:

Dodgers: The player who wins the game becomes the recipient of the "Hatcher Award"—a picture of Dodger Mickey Hatcher's ass.

Rangers: The player who makes the bone-headed fielding play of the day is given a black iron skillet. Taped inside the skillet is a drawing of a glove with the words: "Pete Incaviglia nonstick model."

Expos: The team presents the worst player of the game the "Zilla Award," a Godzilla doll. One of the first recipients of 1987 was pitcher Bryn Smith, who hit an apparent single to right field but was thrown out at first base because he didn't run full speed.

Brewers: Every time they win a game, the players vote on who gets possession of the "John Rambone Award"—an 18-inch-long dildo. "The only national exposure it ever received was when Juan Nieves pitched his no-hitter and the Rambone was hanging behind him in his locker while he was being interviewed," recalls Milwaukee beat writer Tom Flaherty. "General manager Harry Dalton was concerned that one of the TV cameras or still cameras might show it nationally. Harry should have left well enough alone. On one of the newscasts, we saw Nieves talking about his no-hitter when all of a sudden, this huge dildo comes rising up behind him as a hand pulls it out of the way. If Dalton hadn't ordered somebody to move it, the Rambone probably never would have been noticed."

GETTING CARDED

If you walk into a major league clubhouse, you're likely to see signs of a fairly recent trend—baseball cards taped to players' lockers.

Some players display cards of their friends or teammates while pitchers tend to tack up cards of hitters who've homered off of them. "I put up cards of players who hit hard off me," says Dennis Rasmussen of the Yankees. "It's to remind me not to take any hitter for granted." When Reds pitcher Mario Soto decided to put up cards of any hitter who homered off him in 1986, his locker was plastered like a back-alley fence—he served up a league-leading 30 homers. Sometimes, a teammate will tack up a card for the pitcher. "If you give up a homer the day before," says Frank DiPino of the Cubs, "you just might find a card of the guy taped to your locker the next day."

Dodgers hurler Orel Hershiser used to post cards of his fellow teammates and friends Greg Brock, Burt Hooten, and Sid Bream. But now that all three have been released or traded, his other teammates are hoping he won't display any of their cards because it's proving to be an omen of bad luck.

Wherever he goes, Wade Boggs sets up a three-panel frame on the shelf in his locker. The frame contains a baseball card of Boggs on the left, a card of George Brett on the right, and in the middle a photo of the two with their arms around each other. It's labeled "Boggs and his Hero." (Even though the two are close friends, Boggs still calls Brett "Idol" instead of George.)

For years, Glenn Wilson of the Phillies had a baseball card of Lance Parrish taped to his locker because Lance was his best friend when they played together in Detroit. Wilson says he was a rookie when he first met Parrish during spring training. "Parrish came up to me and said, 'Give me your meal money or I'll beat you up.' We've been friends ever since."

♦

FOUL TALK

An observer once said that if you took the seven foulest words out of the English language, ballplayers would have to use sign language. The clubhouse is no place for virgin ears.

"When you're around players every day, it's 'fuck' this and 'motherfucking' that," says Bill Scherrer of the Reds. "It's the language of the baseball fraternity."

Veteran Keith Moreland of the Cubs says he's yet to figure out why men who otherwise seldom swear turn into foulmouths once they set foot in the clubhouse. "It's amazing. Within the realm of the baseball arena, players, managers, coaches, and umpires communicate with each other in language that would be considered foul. Yet away from the clubhouse, most of these same people would never say those words."

For example, Dodgers manager Tommy Lasorda is an eloquent, funny public speaker whose speeches before civic groups are clean as a whistle. Yet he has given the phrase "Dodger blue" a whole new meaning. When Lasorda held a clubhouse meeting midway through the 1987 season to get his struggling team moving in the right direction, he used 130 expletives. "I know because I counted them," said coach Bill Russell, who used a pitch counter to tally the swear words.

"There are a lot of players who swear in the clubhouse but not elsewhere," says Rob Murphy of the Reds. "For example, Dave Parker can speak very articulately, but when he's in the clubhouse, everything is 'motherfucker.' "

Former Brewers manager George Bamberger could turn it on and off, said catcher Bill Schroeder. "Every other word he said was dirty. But whenever there was a woman around, George would be the nicest old guy you'd ever want to meet. He wouldn't even say 'darn.' He was very careful. In fact, his wife didn't even know that he swore until she read newspaper stories about him. His quotes were full of bleeps."

FROM THE DISABLED LIST TO THE CASUALTY LIST

When a member of the Royals goes on the disabled list, he's a true casualty in the eyes of coach Hal McRae.

"McRae gets dressed like a commando, hides in a trash can in the clubhouse, and then jumps out and 'shoots' the guy who's on the DL," says teammate Dan Quisenberry. "McRae believes that if a guy is hurt and can't play, he's dead to the club, so McRae shoots him and kills him."

KANGAROO COURTS

About once or twice a month, a few hours before game time, Pirates coach Rich Donnelly turns into a judge and holds court behind closed clubhouse doors.

Case after case is brought before Donnelly as players testify against each other over some transgression—failing to back up a base, wearing an out-of-style double-knit suit, not bunting a runner over, missing the cutoff man, spending too much time in the hotel lobby. After the testimony in each case is heard, Donnelly renders his "verdict"—which is always "guilty"—and collects another 5-to-10-dollar fine.

Welcome to the Pirates' kangaroo court, typical of the clubhouse jurisprudence practiced throughout the major leagues. It's a way to ease tension and to penalize players a few bucks each time they fail to execute a fundamental play properly.

The Red Sox, under "Judge" Don Baylor, held kangaroo court during their pennant-winning season in 1986. "The court kept the players loose and raised money for a team party and charity," said Roger Clemens. "The court helped make us aware how important it is to execute the little things that win games. Every time I gave up a hit on an 0–2 pitch, I wasn't thinking about the hit so much as I was thinking that I was going to get fined 10 dollars in kangaroo court."

In most kangaroo courts, players who try to plead their case and lose pay double. "And you always lose," says Bruce Hurst of the Red

Sox. "You can hire a teammate to act as legal counsel and present a defense. But there are no good lawyers on our team."

Indians pitcher Sammy Stewart, who used to be Baylor's bailiff at Boston, said Baylor would slap a player with a fine for just about anything. "If you took a teammate out to eat and the food was bad, Don would fine you 25 dollars."

In 1985, when Baylor was the judge for the Yankees' court, pitcher Ron Guidry handed over a check for 100 dollars at the start of the season, said a member of the Yankees. "Guidry told Baylor, 'Just apply this toward the fines you're likely to give me this season.' But Baylor could be nice. If the Yankees had a big lead and the game was dragging and a player hit into a double play, Baylor would give the guy credit toward his next offense since he helped speed up the game."

The highest fine Baylor ever levied was for 100 dollars in 1985. Recalls Baylor, "Normally, if a pitcher gives up a home run on an 0–2 pitch, it's 25 dollars. But Phil Niekro gave up a grand slam on an 0–2 pitch, so he got the maximum fine ever—100 dollars."

Apparently, that made a big impression on Phil Niekro, who has been a merciless kangaroo court judge himself. "In Cleveland in 1986, he was really tough," said Scott Bailes. "He fined me 25 dollars—for being a rookie. Then I got fined another 5 dollars for trying to bring up a case against a teammate. I found out that rookies aren't allowed to bring up cases." When he was judge in Atlanta, Niekro made a big production out of it, said former teammate Bob Walk, of the Phillies. "Phil would hold court in a black robe and white-powdered wig or he'd wear an Uncle Sam outfit—a red, white, and blue suit with a tall hat."

As far as the Cubs are concerned, pitcher Ferguson Jenkins was the toughest clubhouse judge. "He was the most forceful supreme justice I've ever seen," said Keith Moreland. "Nothing slipped by him. For instance, we had a rule that you could talk with someone from the other team before the game for only a couple of minutes. It was called our 'two-minute hello rule.' Fergie would watch us during BP talking to the other team and he would time us. If we went over the limit, we were fined."

Teammate Ryne Sandberg says he'll never forget his first fine from Jenkins. "I had never used a bellhop before in the minors, and when I first got to the majors, I continued to carry my luggage up to my room instead of using the bellhop. Well, a couple of veteran players caught me and I got fined."

Not all teams have or want kangaroo courts. "We had one in 1986," says Jerry Reed of the Mariners, "but it got out of hand. There were so many fines given out that it wasn't fun, but a pain in the butt." The Tigers used to have a court but the players put a stop to it. "Our true feelings are that if you have to run a kangaroo court, you're just looking for bullshit," declares Kirk Gibson. "We think we should be focusing our energies on things that will help us win games."

However, kangaroo courts seem to help young, up-and-coming teams like the Pirates. "It does two things," says Bill Almon, who played for Pittsburgh before moving to the Mets. "First, it reminds you of the basics of the game. It makes you think. Secondly, it builds a camaraderie—everyone getting together with everyone else."

And everyone is fair game—even managers. In 1987, Pittsburgh skipper Jim Leyland was fined for showing up a Pirate batter during BP by catching his fly ball bare-handed. Giants manager Roger Craig was hit up for 10 dollars after he sent in a pinch runner for Harry Spilman, who had just stolen his first base after 410 games. And John McNamara of the Red Sox was fined 25 dollars by Baylor for mistakenly using an aerosol deodorant for hair spray.

JUSTICE, KANGAROO STYLE

Here's a sampling of other verdicts handed down by various kangaroo courts around the major leagues:

Judge Bob Brenly, Giants, 1987: "Brenly fined Matt Williams for getting his first major league hit in 1987 before Brenly was able to get his first hit of the season," said manager Roger Craig.

Judge Andre Dawson, Expos, 1986: "If you were seen talking to an ugly girl, Dawson fined you 50 dollars," said teammate Herm Winningham. "If you were seen talking to her after 11 P.M., he fined you 100 dollars."

Judge Willie Stargell, Braves, 1986: "One of the funniest offenses of the year was committed by Paul Assenmacher, who was then a rookie," said a teammate. "Willie fined him 50 dollars for urinating in the shower, which is considered a big league offense with the Braves."

Judge Don Baylor, Yankees, 1985: "I was running to a base when I tripped," recalls teammate Dave Winfield, "and he fined me 10 dollars for embarrassing the ball club. I appealed and lost, which means I had to pay double. On my way out the door, I kicked over a trash can and a bag of bats and it cost me 5 dollars more. So it cost me 25 dollars for a lousy 10-dollar fine."

Judge Steve Garvey, Padres, 1984: "Luis DeLeon got fined 25 dollars for going to the spread [clubhouse postgame buffet] directly from the shower without a towel," said teammate Tony Gwynn.

Garvey was involved in another celebrated case when he first arrived at spring training in 1983 with his new team, the Padres. "He showed us how very organized and meticulous he is—even in kangaroo court," recalls former teammate Gary Lucas, now with the Angels. "We were coming back from a spring-training game in Phoenix when Garvey had the bus driver drop him off at his condo while the rest of the team had to go on back to club headquarters. That was offensive to us and the team really ragged on Garvey. We took him to kangaroo court and he pleaded guilty—but not without an explanation. He produced a letter written by [Padres vice-president] Jack McKeon, another letter from the bus driver, and a third letter from his mother—all stating that they had given him permission to be dropped off at his home. The letters were all signed and notarized. We were very impressed—and so was the court. Garvey was acquitted."

▲

VETERANS WHO GO OUT OF THEIR WAY TO HELP ROOKIES

1. Nolan Ryan
2. Don Baylor
3. Darrell Evans
4. Willie Randolph
5. Gary Carter

TURNED OFF BY THE TUBE

Television has no place in some clubhouses.

Astros manager Hal Lanier ordered TV sets removed from the Houston clubhouse in 1986 after some of his players skipped infield practice to watch *Wheel of Fortune*.

There has been no TV in the Cardinals' clubhouse since shortly after Whitey Herzog took over as manager in 1980. "They don't need TV," Herzog says. "All they'd watch would be soap operas, game shows, and the NBA."

Herzog doesn't believe in the leniency shown by other managers like the Mets' Davey Johnson, who sometimes allows pitchers into the clubhouse during the game to grab a bite to eat or watch TV. "I have a rule that my pitchers have to be in the dugout," says Herzog. "It seems to me that a starting pitcher wants everybody to bust their butts and root for him when he's pitching, so he ought to be out there rooting for them."

HOW DO HITTERS BABY THEIR BATS?

If you want to tick off a serious hitter, try touching his bat. No possession in the clubhouse is cared for more lovingly than a batter's personal piece of lumber.

Good hitters shower their bats with the TLC they give their wives and children. "During a rain delay this year, Darryl Strawberry took a nap with his bat in the clubhouse." said teammate Roger McDowell. "I also remember when the Pirates were in the World Series in 1979, there was a photo of Dave Parker cuddling his bat like it was a newborn child."

Butch Wynegar of the Angels says no hitter loved his bats more than Jose Morales. "When we played together for the Twins, all he did was DH. I don't think he even owned a glove. He took his bat with him everywhere. Even when he was in the outfield shagging balls during BP, he had his bat. He used to kiss it all the time and would take it back to his hotel room and stand in front of the mirror and swing it. He was a hitter and that was his game."

Chet Lemon of the Tigers often slips his favorite bat into a stretch sanitary sock and takes it back to his hotel room to swing in front of the mirror. Teammate Bill Madlock recalls that when he saw Lemon do this for the first time, "I told Chet, 'You had your chance out there on the field today. There are no hits in that hotel room tonight.' "

Some of the game's top hitters are so protective of their bats that they keep them separate from the rest of the team's lumber. For example, the Phillies' Mike Schmidt, Lance Parrish, and Glenn Wilson each ordered specially made bags to hold their own bats.

"When I played with Boston," recalls Steve Lyons of the White Sox, "Wade Boggs would take his bats to his locker and wouldn't let anybody touch them." That still holds true today. Boggs collects his bats after each game and personally puts them away in his locker. Tim Flannery of the Padres does the same thing. "I keep my bats in my locker because I don't want pitchers to pick one of them up during batting practice and use it and break it."

Although George Brett doesn't baby his bats the way some players do, his lumber is kept under lock and key. "My bats are locked up before and after every series because I've had trouble with people stealing my bats," Brett explains. "I got to Yankee Stadium once with eight bats and played the series there without breaking one of them. Yet when I got to our next stop, Milwaukee, I didn't have a single bat."

The only bat that Brett truly cherishes is the infamous pine-tar bat that triggered a controversy in 1983. "It has seven grains of wood in it and it's my favorite bat," says Brett. "I'll never use it again. It's on display at my restaurant [C. J. Brett's in Hermosa Beach, California] but sometimes I loan it out to Cooperstown."

Brett still loads up the handles of his bats with pine tar, causing Floyd Rayford of the Orioles to declare, "Brett's bats are the ugliest ones I've ever seen. I mean, there is pine tar all over them and they look like they have just been through a war zone."

Many hitters such as Keith Hernandez of the Mets gob sticky substances on the bat handle to get a firm grip. "After every at-bat, Keith has the trainer rub his bat handle down with alcohol," said Mets coach Bill Robinson. "Then he puts fresh stick-um on it before his next at-bat."

Using rubbing alcohol on bats is a common practice for hitters who pay particular attention to the marks that balls leave on the bat when there's contact. "When you hit the ball, a mark will show on the bat," explains White Sox coach Ed Brinkman. "By looking at the marks, you can get an idea whether you're hitting on the end of the bat, or near the handle, or right on the joy spot. I know Pete Rose used to wipe all the marks off his bat after each game so he could see where he was hitting the ball."

Batters' use of alcohol on their bats depends on how well they are hitting, says Gary Redus of the White Sox. "If you're going good, you clean up your bat with alcohol right after the game. But if you're going bad, you just leave it alone."

Mike Easler of the Yankees says he not only puts alcohol on his bats, but he rubs them with a ham bone to keep them from chipping. "I used to bone my bat a lot," says Butch Wynegar. "I had a foot-long bone that I rubbed on the grain to make it harder, but I haven't done that in a long time. In Chicago, there's a stand in the clubhouse where you can bone your bat, but you don't see many players boning bats."

However, you do see hitters shaving or sanding their bats. "Ray Knight is always sanding and scraping the handles of his bats to get just the right feel," says teammate Terry Kennedy of the Orioles. "He also scrapes his bats because he doesn't want to get too much buildup of tar on the handles."

Some players become almost obsessive over shaving bats. Says Dan Plesac of the Brewers, "You could put me in a clubhouse blindfolded and all I'd need to hear is *whoosh, whoosh, whoosh* and I'd know it's Rob Deer. He's always shaving his bat handles down. I mean, it's incredible. If you see him sitting next to his locker without a razor shaving down the handles, he almost looks naked."

It's one thing for hitters to care about their bats, but pitchers? Some of the Phillies poke fun at pitcher Kent Tekulve for sanding the barrels of his bats. "He tries to flatten the bat somewhat because he thinks it will help him lay down a better bunt, but I don't think it does," says teammate Darren Daulton.

Blue Jays hitting star George Bell shaves his bats until they are precisely the weight he wants, says teammate Lloyd Moseby. "They all have to be exactly the same."

According to Wynegar, former teammate and batting champ Rod Carew, who retired after the 1985 season, was even fussier. "He was so particular that he used to weigh his bats in the clubhouse, and if they were only two grams underweight, he wouldn't use them."

▲

GLOVE AFFAIR

A fielder's glove is not only an extension of his hand but of his personality.

"I think every player treats his glove as if it were a piece of his body," says Ed Vande Berg of the Indians. "Just as everybody has his own style of combing his hair, everybody has his own way of treating his glove."

Like most fielders, Buddy Biancalana of the Royals doesn't want anyone to touch his glove. "I like a tight-fitting glove and it has to feel right every time I put it on. If someone else puts on my glove, it can stretch the inside fit of the fingers. If I see someone putting on my glove, I get on him and order him to take it off. He might think I'm kidding at first, but I'm dead serious."

All-Star shortstop Tony Fernandez of the Blue Jays takes extra special care of his game glove, says teammate Lloyd Moseby. "He'll use anybody else's glove during infield practice, but never his own. He wouldn't think of using his game glove for practice. It's strictly for when it counts."

Fernandez's All-Star counterpart in the National League, Ozzie Smith of the Cardinals, won't play with any glove other than a formerly discontinued model called the Trap-Eze. Instead of a webbing between the thumb and forefinger, the leather of the palm extends upward into that space like a sixth finger. When Smith was a rookie in 1978, he was still using the same glove he had worn since junior high school. But by the time he made it to the major leagues, the pocket of his glove had ripped out. Even though the manufacturer had discontinued the line, Smith convinced the company to make him another one. "Shortly after that, I won my first Gold Glove and now everybody is using that model," he said.

Every fielder, it seems, has his own way of breaking in a new glove. Red Sox catcher Rich Gedman says the first thing he does with a new mitt is put it in water and beat it down with a bat. "Then I tape two balls together, put them in the glove, tape the glove down over the balls, and let it dry out."

Dwight Evans of the Red Sox says his gloves must go through lengthy apprenticeships before they ever make it into a game. He begins breaking in a new glove during spring training and then only uses it in practice or when playing catch or shagging fly balls. The glove won't get into a spring-training game until the following year and may not see major league action for several seasons after that.

Evans, who set an outfielders' record of 192 games of errorless ball in 1973–74, claims he would have extended his flawless streak if only his glove hadn't been stolen. "I didn't have another glove ready and I played another 10 games with one that was too new. Finally, in Chicago, I made two errors in one game and I was shaking."

Lloyd Moseby can sympathize with Evans. "I played with one glove for three years," said Moseby, "and I had so much confidence in it that when it finally went down, it was like a burial of some sort. Your glove is a friend and you get so comfortable with it that you just don't want to give it up."

To keep his glove in perfect shape and extend its life, Cal Ripkin, Jr., of the Orioles says he puts Vaseline in the fingers every few games to keep them from getting too hard. His teammate, Floyd Rayford, thinks some fielders have gone to the extreme. "A lot of guys won't even dust off home plate or a base with their glove because they say you make your living with your glove and you don't want to get it any dirtier than you have to. That's going too far."

That's not too far at all compared to what Expos reserve infielder Rene Gonzalez does. "He keeps one of his gloves in a Wonder Bread wrapper," says teammate Bryn Smith. "His reasoning is that since Wonder Bread has no holes, neither will his glove."

WEIRD THINGS PLAYERS DO TO THEIR EQUIPMENT

Ozzie Guillen, White Sox: "When I struggle at the plate, I ask the trainer for eye drops and I put them right on my bat so my bat can see the ball good. I also talk to my glove when I make an error. I say, 'What's going on? Do you feel tired? Talk to me. Let me know what's wrong with you.' "

Tom Brookens, Detroit Tigers light-hitting infielder: "I scuffed my bat just to make it look like I hit the ball."

Milt Thompson, Phillies: "[Teammate] Luis Aguayo takes magic markers and colors his gloves, even the laces."

Pete O'Brien, Rangers: "[Teammate] Mike Stanley puts the letters H-O-T-B on the knob of his bat handle. It's a key to remind him to keep his head on the ball; in other words, keep your head down and hit through the ball."

Jim Fregosi, White Sox manager and former player: "I was in an awful slump and I went to see Dr. [Robert] Kerlan and said, 'You gotta give my bat a shot.' He filled a syringe with cortisone and injected it in my bat. The first time I popped up. Clete Boyer was playing third base, and the ball hit off his glove and he dropped it. I hit for the cycle that day."

▲

WHAT STRANGE CLUBHOUSE ROUTINES DO PLAYERS FOLLOW BEFORE EACH GAME?

When not reading fan mail or signing baseballs, many players engage in pregame rituals to relax themselves or get psyched up.

Glenn Davis of the Astros meditates—in the bathroom. "He doesn't go to the bathroom, he just sits there for twenty minutes and meditates," says a teammate.

Some players relax by eating snacks before games. "Dave Smith [of the Astros] is probably the most laid-back player I've ever seen," says his former teammate Bill Dawley of the Cardinals. "He'll eat a couple of pieces of pizza or a cheeseburger five or ten minutes before the game and then go down to the bullpen during the middle innings."

Before every home game, Angels manager Gene Mauch has the clubhouse boy deliver him half of a frozen Snickers bar and a glass of milk, says Los Angeles beat writer Peter Schmuck. "It's delivered like clockwork at a designated time."

When Joe Niekro was with the Astros, he always had coffee with a used-car salesman before every start at home. Keith Hernandez of the Mets likes to sit alone at a clubhouse table with a cup of black coffee and a cigarette. Blue Jays hurler Dave Stieb eats a tuna sandwich before he starts.

It's not unusual for players to act differently on days they've been penciled into the lineup. "When [Angels outfielder] Ruppert Jones is not playing, he's very outgoing, talkative, and fun to be around," says teammate Gary Lucas. "But when he's going to play that day, he's very quiet and hard to find. Usually, he's somewhere in a little room behind the training room, meditating." Adds teammate DeWayne Buice, "Rupert goes into a corner, puts on his headphones, lays down on the concrete, and totally vegetates for a couple of hours."

Of all the pregame pastimes, none is more popular than card playing, especially in the Orioles, Brewers, and Royals clubhouses. "Every day, there are about 10 guys who want to play bridge," says Bret Saberhagen of the Royals. "They get two games going while two of the players have to wait until someone quits. It's a race to see who gets there first so they don't get shut out from playing bridge. I don't see why anyone would come to the ball park five hours early just to play bridge. It can't be that much fun."

The Brewers also play bridge—and gin, pinochle, poker, and pluck. "The Brewers are a very difficult team to interview in the clubhouse before the game," says Milwaukee beat writer Tom Flaherty. "Almost everybody is playing cards."

In the Twins clubhouse, one of the eagerly awaited events of the day is watching All-Star outfielder Kirby Puckett shave his head. "He only does it if he had an 0-for game the previous day," says former teammate Ron Davis of the Cubs. "The Twins love it, especially after he's been on a hitting streak and it's been a while since he shaved. When he does shave it off, the players rub his head for good luck."

While the vast majority of players engage in some sort of pregame routine, few have any postgame rituals other than quaffing a few beers after their shower to wind down. However, there are some exceptions.

Angels veteran pitcher Don Sutton ices his whole body after he pitches. "He sits in an ice bath for twenty minutes because he says it has a rejuvenating effect on him," says Peter Schmuck. "Then he takes care of his postgame interviews. He always looks like he has frostbite and is shivering during the interviews. Another veteran Angel, Bob Boone, lifts weights in the clubhouse after the game and then runs one to two miles even on the hottest, most humid days. He does this after squatting maybe 200 times while catching during the game."

Rob Murphy of the Reds has his own postgame ritual, which he says never varies. "I shower the same way every day and never break the routine. Crotch first, right leg, left leg, stomach, chest, right armpit, left armpit, right arm, left arm, back, face, neck, and then shampoo."

▲

PREGAME RITUALS OF STARTING PITCHERS

Danny Jackson, Royals—He mentally prepares himself by listening to inspirational music—"Eye of the Tiger" by Survivor and the soundtrack of the movie *Rocky IV.* Sitting at his locker, Jackson dons his headphones, closes his eyes, and grooves on the music for hours, says teammate Bud Black. "He's more or less in his own world."

Steve Trout, Yankees—He conducts his own private meditation ceremony in front of his locker. "He goes through yoga exercises to get himself psyched up," says a teammate. "Steve looks straight ahead, breathes deeply, and stands on one foot. Some of the guys look at him with raised eyebrows and wonder about him."

George Riley, Giants—When he was slated to pitch, "he wouldn't talk to anyone from the time he got up in the morning until after the game," said the Phillies' Don Carman. "George would show up at the clubhouse, go find a corner, curl up in the fetal position, and not say a word to anyone. If you tried to talk to him, he'd just wave you off. When it was time to warm up, he'd first have a cigarette and then go out onto the field."

Dave Stewart, Athletics—He waits until the last possible minute to get ready. "He doesn't put his uniform on until right before he has to go out and warm up," says a teammate. "He likes to stay in his street clothes."

Ron Darling, Terry Leach, Dwight Gooden, Mets—The Mets starting pitchers all have different pregame rituals on days they are scheduled to pitch, says coach Mel Stottlemyre. "Some of the guys like to hide in the clubhouse on game day and mentally prepare. Ron Darling becomes pretty invisible. But Terry Leach likes to shag fly balls in the outfield because he doesn't want to be left alone in the clubhouse. Dwight Gooden enjoys playing cards before he pitches. He tries especially hard to win at cards because he thinks it will bring him good luck on the mound."

Frank Pastore, Twins—In 1986, Pastore drew plenty of stares from his teammates by engaging in an hour-long martial-arts routine. After doing squats, sit-ups, and push-ups, he kicked his way around the clubhouse.

Bill Wegman, Brewers—Wegman acts like Dr. Jekyll and Mr. Hyde in the hours before he pitches, claims teammate Bill Schroeder. "I mean, four days a week he's running around the clubhouse like a nut, having fun and joking around. On the day he pitches, he comes in and sits down by his locker without saying a word. He looks like he has lost his best friend. We get on him about it, but he says it's his game plan and it works for him."

THE NEVER-CHANGING PREGAME RITUAL OF WADE BOGGS

No player in the majors follows a pregame ritual with more precision and dedication than Wade Boggs of the Red Sox.

The routine begins at home at 2 P.M. when he sits down with his family for a daily chicken dinner. (Boggs has been eating chicken every day since he noticed in the minors that he always seemed to hit best after a chicken meal.)

Boggs arrives at the clubhouse about 3:15 P.M. every day and sits down in front of his locker at precisely 3:30 P.M. and begins to get into his uniform. At 4 P.M., he goes to the dugout and sits down. At 4:10 P.M., he plays catch and then takes ground balls for about 20 minutes.

Next, Boggs goes out to center field and begins mentally preparing himself for the game. "I think about who's pitching and how they're going to play me," he says. "And I relax. Then I'm ready to take batting practice." Before taking infield practice, Boggs stands in the dugout runway and throws the ball against the wall for five minutes.

Finally, he starts running wind sprints at exactly 7:17 P.M., not a minute earlier or later. (When Bobby Cox was managing the Blue Jays, he once tried to foul up Boggs's routine by having the Exhibition Stadium clock go from 7:16 to 7:18, but Boggs wasn't fooled.) Asked if he would postpone his wind sprints if the President phoned him at 7:17 P.M., Boggs replied, "I'd put the White House on hold. Hey, I've got my priorities."

▲

FORGERY IN THE CLUBHOUSE

You might want to take a close look at that baseball sitting on your shelf; you know, the ball with all the signatures of players on your favorite team. There's a good chance that some of those autographs were forged.

Before almost every game, clubbies (clubhouse attendants) place boxes of baseballs on the clubhouse table and ask the players to sign them. Half-dressed players with a few minutes to spare scribble their signatures on one ball after another before the balls are taken away and sold or, in special cases, given away. However, not all players sign them. Some are lazy or forget or promise to sign later and never do. As a result, someone else forges their name.

"The practice is a whole lot more common than you think," says Jerry Reed of the Mariners. "There are usually three or four dozen balls sitting on the table every day to get signed. The clubbies will say, 'Can you sign the balls?' And you answer, 'You just go ahead and sign my name.' "

The vast majority of players allows this type of forgery to flourish, claims a Yankee. "You see it happen all the time. Every baseball must be suspect and that's unfortunate." Adds an Angel, "The more requests you get, the more you try to find someone to help you sign balls. Realistically, how many players can afford to take the time to sign all those balls? We've got too much fan mail as it is."

The bigger the star, the more likely his signature is forged, said another Angel. "Players usually sign balls during the first few months of their careers, but the novelty soon wears off. Then if you're a superstar like Reggie Jackson and your autograph is in demand, you find someone to help sign your name. That's what Reggie does."

Front offices use clubbies or mail-room people to forge signatures of popular players. "The best clubhouse man for forging baseballs is in Philadelphia," says a Phillie. "He is the greatest. You'd never know the signature was a fake. He can sign Schmitty's [Mike Schmidt's] name perfectly. He did Lefty's [Steve Carlton's] too."

Players often help each other out. "Julio Cruz [of the White Sox] would sign his teammates' names to balls," said a former teammate. "He was terrific as a forger."

Bill Dawley of the Cardinals claims he's never seen any forged signatures—especially his. "No one could forge mine anyway because it looks like chicken scratch."

According to a Brave, clubhouse forgery has all but disappeared in Atlanta since the arrival of manager Chuck Tanner. "If anything, Tanner is Mr. Baseball. He still believes in the purity of the game."

FATHER DOESN'T KNOW BEST

Most every team has rules prohibiting or limiting players' children, wives, and friends from coming into the clubhouse—often with good reason.

In 1986, the father of Indians rookie Cory Snyder was kicked out of the clubhouse for good by manager Pat Corrales. Recalls a member of the Indians:

"Snyder's father would stand behind the batting cage during BP and yell at him, 'Put your hands closer! Get your arms together! Get your wrists loose! Extend your arms!' Then he'd be coaching him in the clubhouse every day.

"Finally, Pat held a closed-door meeting with Cory's father and told him, 'Look, you've done a very good job of working with him and preparing him to be a major league player. But now it's time for you to step away. It's my turn. I never want to see you in here again. If you don't believe me, there are 40 guys in the clubhouse who will make life hell for your son. How many other fathers do you see in here?' Cory's father understood and never went into the clubhouse after that."

HOW DO PLAYERS PASS THE TIME DURING RAIN DELAYS?

Aside from the usual things like playing cards, reading, answering fan mail, or napping, some players have found other ways to while away the time during rain delays. For example:

Mark Gubicza, Royals: "Sometimes Sabes [Bret Saberhagen] and I will play hockey in the clubhouse. I'm the goalie and I try to defend my locker using my mitt as a hockey glove and a bat as my goalie stick. Sabes uses a bat as his stick and a ball for a puck."

Roger McDowell, Mets: "We make a ball out of tape and hit it with a fungo bat and the other guys try to catch it."

Ken Schrom, Indians: "When I was with Minnesota, we played Hackeysack [a foot-bag game] for almost two hours during a rain delay. We were sweating bullets and got so worn out that we were almost too tired to play baseball."

Cal Ripkin, Jr., Orioles: "I watch the rain and eat sunflower seeds. If we're losing early in the game, I try to keep it raining with my mind, and if we're ahead late in the game, then I try to make it stop."

WHO ARE THE BIGGEST MEDIA HOGS IN BASEBALL?

1. **Reggie Jackson**
2. **Gary Carter**
3. **Don Sutton**

Rangers manager Bobby Valentine always tells his players, "Get your name in the papers whenever you can—good or bad. That's what makes this game."

Maybe so. But some players go out of their way to give reporters unwanted quotes and seek cameras and microphones the way a beagle sniffs out a raccoon.

"The all-time champion media hog is Reggie Jackson," declares a teammate. "Once he stopped hitting 30 homers a season, he began stealing the limelight from his teammates. Every time a player has an exceptional performance—two homers or a shutout—Reggie always finds a way to sneak into the press gathering around that player."

Los Angeles beat writer Peter Schmuck concurs. "When [Angels reliever] Donnie Moore was tearing up the league with 31 saves in 1985, Reggie was with him constantly whenever he was interviewed. In 1986, Wally Joyner emerged as a Rookie of the Year candidate for the Angels and was the first rookie ever to be elected to the All-Star Game. The player who spent the most time with him when he was being interviewed was Reggie and some of his teammates complained about it."

When Jackson joined the Athletics in 1987, he tried to capture some of the limelight from A's rookie sensation Mark McGwire, said Ron Kittle of the Yankees. "Reggie survives on media attention. When McGwire hit five homers in two days, Reggie jumped right in there and tried to give him advice in the newspapers. It wasn't a situation where his advice was needed."

There's a fine line between being an accommodating player and being a media hog. To some, Gary Carter of the Mets is the former; to others, he's the latter. "Gary will show up for an interview even if he's 0 for 54," says teammate Tim Teufel. Adds Montreal beat writer

Wesley Goldstein, "Gary Carter is the kind of person whom you ask a question, hand him a tape recorder, and come back 20 minutes later. He doesn't stop talking."

In Montreal, they call him "Camcorder Carter," claims another reporter. "Gary knows where the camera is at all times. He seems to have a sixth sense for when the camera is on him." And that has bugged Rob Murphy of the Reds, who said, "In the 1986 Series, every time there was a camera shot in the dugout, Gary Carter knew about it and mugged it up."

Angels hurler Don Sutton has bugged many of his teammates in his quest for the limelight, says an Astro. "When Sutton was with us, there was a standing joke among us: 'If you can't find Sutton and don't know where he is, just look in front of the nearest camera.' " According to another former teammate, Sutton actually sneaked out of the stadium during a game in Atlanta and went into the television truck hoping to get on the air.

"Sutton will go out of his way to get on TV," said a California reporter. "He'll come in from deep center field during batting practice just to see if he can be interviewed for television. Sure, it's appreciated by the TV people, but his teammates are getting tired of him always putting himself first."

According to the *Baseball Confidential* survey, two young up-and-coming media hogs are Charlie Kerfeld of the Astros and Joe Magrane of the Cardinals. "Kerfeld will say any outrageous thing just to get his name in the papers," says a teammate. Adds Bill Dawley of the Cardinals, who has played with both players, "Charlie always tries to get his quote of the day in the paper or on the radio. And Magrane loves coming up with lines for the press."

Some sample quotes from Charlie Kerfeld:

- "Of course I'm a good role model for kids because I'm an outstanding model citizen of America."
- "If I ever get married, all the beautiful women will be happy and all the ugly, fat ones will be pissed."

Some sample quotes from Joe Magrane:

- "After all the X rays [on his elbow], my fastball may take on an opaque-type glow."

- "I knew I was in big trouble when they started clocking my fastball with a sundial."
- "I passed the time by reading a book. It was called *JFK: The Man and the Airport.*"

HOW PLAYERS MESS WITH THE PRESS

Most players maintain a decent relationship with sports writers. However, some players have the same gut feeling toward the media as they do toward an accidental swallow of tobacco juice. Usually, they refuse to talk to reporters. Sometimes they hassle them. On rare occasions they assault them.

With the 1986 retirement of hothead John Denny, clubhouse altercations with reporters have diminished. But reporters and players alike admit that some loutish players could learn a few manners. "By far the worst thing I've ever seen was when Julio Gonzalez [of the Astros] grabbed a note pad away from a reporter and proceeded to urinate on it," said a former teammate. "Usually, the bad things you see now are some screaming and shouting and swearing."

In the middle of the 1987 season when the press was writing about the internal squabbling, bitterness, and discontent that permeated the Mets' clubhouse, several players took matters in their own hands. While reporters were interviewing pitcher Terry Leach, a player tossed a firecracker at the sportswriters. Then some of the players hurled dirty socks and underwear at the scribes.

Some players like George Hendrick of the Angels follow a standing policy not to talk to the press—and reporters respect their wishes. What the media finds bush are players who only talk when they've had a good game.

"George Hendrick hasn't talked to the media since 1974," says Los Angeles beat writer Peter Schmuck. "The funny thing is, he's the friendliest player on the team toward reporters, as long as they don't have a microphone or a notebook sticking in his face. He just doesn't feel comfortable talking to the press and we understand. Unfortunately, he cheats himself out of the recognition he deserves."

But some players with chips on their shoulders shut out reporters to punish them for some perceived injustice. "Mike Witt [of the

Angels] doesn't enjoy talking to the local media because he feels he got burned in his early years with the club," Schmuck explains. "The coaching staff was critical of him when he was young and that showed up in print. He feels he was treated too harshly by the media. In 1986, when he won 18 games, Witt went out of his way to be unfriendly to reporters. At one point, a reporter asked him, 'Why not leave it all behind and start fresh?' And Witt said, 'No. Maybe next year I'll have a bad year and it will be your turn to be unfriendly.' It's really sad because he grew up in the Anaheim area. He could really be a hometown hero. Until the 1986 playoffs, there wasn't one full-sized feature about him in any southern California newspaper because he's so truculent."

Cubs reliever Ray Fontenot had such disdain for reporters that he was always telling them off, says Chicago beat writer Fred Mitchell. "In 1986, after one of his rare wins, Fontenot told reporters, 'You can kiss my ass. I have nothing to say to you guys. You ripped me when I wasn't going well and I'm not going to say anything now to help you guys out.' This type of behavior did not endear him to his teammates. Once, when Fontenot was hiding in the shower for 45 minutes waiting for reporters to leave, one of the Cubs said, 'Who does he think he is, a 30-game winner? He hasn't won 30 games in his career.' "

Some players enjoy poking fun at members of the media whose reporting skills are as suspect as the batting eye of a .200 hitter. For example, if Jim Deshaies of the Astros thinks a reporter has asked him a stupid question, the pitcher hits the button on a laugh machine.

More than once, Doug DeCinces of the Angels has started fake-trade rumors that made it into print. "Reggie [Jackson], Bob Boone, and I started one about Bobby Grich and it worked so well that the front office issued a statement denying it, which gave it great credibility," said DeCinces. "The reporters were writing about it for a week. Then [in 1987], Boone, Brian Downing, and I started one about the Dodgers trading Mike Marshall, Ken Howell, and Alejandro Pena to Baltimore for Eddie Murray. Radio reporters spent all night trying to confirm it and [Angels manager] Gene Mauch had 15 reporters asking him about it. We were all busting up laughing. It just goes to show you that you can't believe everything you read in the papers."

Players show no mercy toward ill-prepared reporters. The Yankees played a hoax on a *Time* magazine reporter in 1987. The reporter, obviously out of his element, asked one of the players to point out "Tom" Mattingly. The player pointed to Mike Pagliarulo. The reporter then spent 20 minutes talking to Pags, who obliged him with phony answers. Later, another reporter informed the man from *Time* that he had been duped.

In 1986, after Royals pitcher Dennis Leonard pitched a complete game in a 2-1 loss to Detroit, teammate Dan Quisenberry was sitting in front of Leonard's locker while Leonard was in the trainer's room. Two unsuspecting Detroit radio reporters thrust microphones in Quiz's face, thinking he was Leonard. They asked him about his comeback from knee surgery, how it felt to throw a two-hitter and lose, and if he considered his comeback a medical miracle. Quisenberry politely answered all of the questions. He didn't even crack a smile—until the reporters left to play their interviews over the air.

▲

WHY YOU SHOULDN'T BELIEVE EVERYTHING IN THE SPORTS PAGES

Blue Jays star Jesse Barfield says he won't joke with the press anymore without making sure the reporters know he's just pulling their leg.

"One time I dropped a fly ball in Milwaukee and, after the game, the writers asked me what happened," he recalled. "I told them, 'Well, I was looking up and a UFO flew right across. It was weird. I never saw anything like that in my life.' Man, I was only joking and they wrote it up and put it in the paper."

▲

NO WAY TO TREAT A LADY

Even though it's the policy of major league baseball to allow women reporters in the clubhouse, many players remain outraged—and some go out of their way to hassle women.

"When the clubhouses were first opened to women, there were players who tried to offend them by bringing in sex aids," says a veteran beat writer. "I saw some Dodgers appear to fondle themselves in front of women reporters. Reggie Jackson would completely undress and stay that way while drinking a Moosehead beer. He's so proud of his body and it's obvious that he was posing and showing it off. That kind of stuff is less common now than it used to be."

But women reporters contend they still must battle crude and offensive treatment by players who want the clubhouse to remain a male bastion. For instance, Steve Sax of the Dodgers pulled a joke designed to upset a woman reporter in Montreal in 1985, says Montreal beat writer Wesley Goldstein. "All of us reporters were interviewing Jerry Reuss, who had just shut out the Expos. One of the reporters was a woman named Sandy Rubin of radio station CKO in Montreal. She was in front of the crowd holding a microphone as Reuss answered questions by his locker in his underwear. All of a sudden, Sax pushed his way through the crowd and he was wearing nothing but a sock over his penis." Recalls Rubin, "Sax walked right up to me and then wiggled the lower part of his body and shouted, 'Sock it to me! Sock it to me!' I just ignored him."

Reporter Lisa Dillman of *The Detroit News* was disgusted by remarks Tigers star Kirk Gibson made to her when she first entered the clubhouse in 1984. "Gibson said the only reason she was there was to gaze at a certain part of the players' bodies," recalls Detroit beat writer Vern Plagenhoef. "Of course, Gibson put it in much stronger language than that, but he subsequently had to write her an apology. There have been a couple of incidents like that. Whenever a woman reporter comes into the clubhouse, Gibson has a favorite expression. He shouts: 'Clams in the clubhouse!' "

The Braves allow women reporters in the clubhouse but that doesn't mean the players talk to them. "When a woman enters the clubhouse after a game, many of the Braves retreat into the training room where no members of the media are allowed," says Atlanta beat reporter Joe Strauss. "The players just wait it out until the female reporter leaves. Dale Murphy, because of his Mormon beliefs, will even take his clothes in the training room and get dressed and leave without talking to anybody if there's a female in the room. The Braves have been cited several times by the league office for this attitude. So the team does comply, but nobody is going to make them talk to women [in the clubhouse]."

Glenn Hubbard of the Braves, echoing the feeling of many of his teammates, says, "I will not talk to a woman reporter in the clubhouse. I will go out of my way to let her know that too. I just don't think it's right."

WHAT ARE THE DUMBEST QUESTIONS SPORTSWRITERS COMMONLY ASK?

Bill Madlock, Tigers: "When I make an error and they ask 'Why did that happen?' I feel like answering, 'I made it on purpose because I want our team to lose.'"

Donnie Moore, Angels: "After I give up a home run that goes 500 fucking miles and the reporter asks, 'Was it a good pitch?' That's stupid. A batter doesn't hit a good pitch 500 fucking feet."

Kent Tekulve, Phillies: "There's so many, it's hard to pick out one. A dumb one is 'Why did you give up that home run?' Sometimes I'll answer, 'Because I felt like it.' There's no way you can answer a question like that."

Bob Walk, Pirates: "When I've been shelled and the reporter asks me, 'What happened?' or 'How do you feel?' I usually say, 'How the hell do you think I feel? You saw what happened.' That's when there's trouble. The pitcher is in the wrong frame of mind and all it takes is a dumb question to set him off."

Mark Clear, Brewers: "After giving up a big homer and being asked, 'What was the problem out there tonight?' or 'Did you throw the ball where you wanted to?'"

THE
BASE
PATHS

WHO ARE THE MAJOR LEAGUES' MOST DARING BASE RUNNERS?

1. **Alfredo Griffin**
2. **Rickey Henderson**
3. **Vince Coleman**
4. **Willie Wilson**

They are more than just speed merchants. They are the daredevils of the base paths, running on bravado as much as talent to make things happen.

Alfredo Griffin, the swift, exciting shortstop for the Athletics, rates as the most daring base runner in the bigs, according to the *Baseball Confidential* survey. "He's intimidating on the base paths because you never know what he's going to do," says teammate Carney Lansford. "Heck, even his own team doesn't know what he's going to do."

Ron Washington of the Orioles calls Griffin the smartest runner in the game today. "The other day he took third base on a throw from the catcher back to the pitcher. I've seen Griffin steal home on the very same type of throw."

Griffin anticipates the play before it happens, says Mickey Tettleton of the A's. "He's able to take an extra base or score a run when one shouldn't be scored—like that night in Seattle in 1986." In that game, Griffin was on second base with a teammate on first when Mariners pitcher Mike Moore walked the next batter to load the bases. Moore was so disgusted that he angrily caught the throwback from catcher Steve Yeager, turned his back to the plate, and stalked off the mound. Meanwhile, Griffin rounded third and never stopped. By the time Moore wheeled around and threw to the plate, it was too late. Griffin had scored.

For sheer quickness, the players' nod goes to Rickey Henderson of the Yankees. "You look at him at first base and you know he has it in his mind to steal off you," says Royals pitcher Mark Gubicza. "So you hope you get lucky and that he stumbles or something on his way to second."

Even when you think you've picked him off, Henderson finds a way to beat you. "There was a game last year in New York when I picked him off three times—and never got him out," recalls Scott McGregor of the Orioles. "We either threw it away in a rundown or he just kept running and beat the throw to second. He's pretty tough."

He's cocky too. In a recent game, Floyd Rayford was playing third for the Orioles and Henderson was dancing off first. "He looked across the diamond at me and held up two fingers," Rayford said. "I didn't know what he meant until two pitches later when he was standing on third base with back-to-back steals."

Ever since he burst on the scene in 1985, Vince Coleman of the Cardinals has owned the base paths as the number-one thief in baseball. "If there's one guy I hate to see on base, it's Coleman," said a veteran hurler. "A walk to him is like giving up a double or a triple. He can sure rattle you."

Coleman broke the major league record for steals by a rookie when he swiped his 73rd and 74th bases—on the same play. During a game against the Cubs, Coleman dove headfirst into third on the front end of a double steal, but he overslid the bag. So he simply got up and headed for home. Third baseman Ron Cey threw to catcher Jody Davis, who ran Coleman back toward third and threw to Cey. Coleman reversed his direction, ran past Davis, and scored.

Also highly rated for his base-running skills is Willie Wilson of the Royals. "He always looks for ways to take the extra base," says Dan Quisenberry of the Royals. "You very seldom see him get caught. He's just so heads-up." Says a Yankee pitcher, "He's one of those rare runners who seems to get better with age. I hate to see him on base."

NAILING THE RUNNER

White Sox shortstop Ozzie Guillen made the easiest putout of his career in 1985. He tagged the Royals' Willie Wilson, who had been knocked out by Carlton Fisk's throw on an attempted steal.

"I was just doing my job," said Guillen. "I had to do it fast, or the trainer would have come out and they'd have called time."

Fisk said it was the first time he had thrown out Wilson. "And I had to knock him out to do it."

WHAT PLAYERS ARE BEST AT DECOYING BASE RUNNERS?

1. **Ozzie Guillen**
2. **Ozzie Smith**
3. **Mike Schmidt**
4. **Marty Barrett**
5. **Alfredo Griffin**
6. **Jim Rice**

The "Wizards of Oz"—shortstops Ozzie Guillen of the White Sox and Ozzie Smith of the Cardinals—conjure up the best illusions to deke runners.

"Guillen is always doing something to take out the runners," says Terry Kennedy of the Orioles. "If you're running to second and don't pick the ball up off the bat, then he's got a chance of getting you. He'll say something to make you think a hit is a fly ball or he'll pretend to catch a throw at second when there isn't even a play just to make you slide and keep you from going to third on a hit. He's good, very good."

As runners, Alan Trammell, Steve Buechele, Rudy Law, and Lloyd Moseby have all been duped by Guillen. "I was terribly embarrassed by Ozzie," admits Moseby. During a 1987 game in Chicago, Moseby broke for second on the pitch. Catcher Carlton Fisk's throw sailed into center field, giving Moseby what appeared to be an easy stolen base. But he was fooled by Guillen, who shouted to second baseman Freddy Manrique, "It's a pop-up. Throw the ball to first." Moseby got up from his slide into second and scampered back toward first. (Actually, he ended up again at second because the throw to first from the center fielder was wild.)

"Ozzie Guillen is always up to something," says Bret Saberhagen of the Royals. "He'll sneak in behind a runner leading off second and toss some dirt to the guy's right. The runner will look to his right while Guillen runs to the bag to take the pickoff throw. He's fun to watch."

Ozzie Smith's favorite ploy is deking runners trying to steal second. "He got me a couple of times when I was in the National League," says Gary Redus of the White Sox. "The last time, I was trying to steal second and I really didn't look at the plate to see where the ball was. I was watching Ozzie, who was just standing there on the bag holding up his hand to me like the ball wasn't coming. I slowed down just enough for him to quickly catch the ball and tag me out."

Veteran third baseman Mike Schmidt of the Phillies is considered the best at faking throws and hanging up runners. "He creates outs that shouldn't happen," says a rival infielder. "He's excellent at deking the runner, and even though he's been doing it for years, he still nails them." Schmidt usually targets the runner on second. When a ground ball is hit to him, Schmidt will fake the throw to first and then trap the runner off second.

Marty Barrett of the Red Sox and Alfredo Griffin of the Athletics specialize in decoying runners on first from going to third on a single. "On those humpback pop-ups that Marty knows he or the outfielder can't catch, he'll backpedal and pretend he has it all the way," says Lenn Sakata of the Yankees. "The ball drops in for a hit and the runner on first is lucky to make it safely to second when he should have made it to third."

Griffin loves to thwart hit-and-run plays. "He deked me once," said a Twins player. "I was on first and took off on the hit-and-run. The guy behind me singled, but I didn't see it. Griffin acted like it was a ground ball and he came across the bag, pretending to be the pivot man on a double play and got me to slide. I would have made it to third easily if I hadn't been deked."

Other infielders highly rated for their skill at decoying runners include Bill Doran of the Astros, Ryne Sandberg of the Cubs, Tony Fernandez of the Blue Jays, Alan Trammell of the Tigers, and Frank White of the Royals.

However, infielders don't have a lock on deking. According to the survey, Red Sox left fielder Jim Rice has faked out plenty of runners. "He tried to deke me last year and I would have fallen for it if I hadn't seen him do it a few times before," said Rob Deer of the Brewers. "He usually tries it in Fenway Park with its short wall. He pretends like he's going to catch the ball to freeze the runner and then at the last second he turns his back on the runner and plays the ball off the wall. He's a good actor."

THE HIDDEN BALL TRICK

Of all the decoys perpetrated by infielders, none is harder to pull off—or enjoyed more—than the hidden ball trick. You would think that major leaguers couldn't possibly fall for this Little League ploy. Yet this sneaky scam still claims a runner every now and then.

Two of the best at carrying out this piece of chicanery are Red Sox second baseman Marty Barrett and Tigers first baseman Dave Bergman.

The pinnacle of Barrett's career as a hidden ball trick artist came in 1985 when he bamboozled two Angel runners within a two-week period. "The first time it happened was after Bobby Grich had been bunted over to second," recalls Barrett. "I had fielded the bunt but couldn't make a play to first or second, so I held the ball. The first-base coach was congratulating the batter and the third-base coach was looking in at the manager for a sign, so I figured this was the perfect time to try the hidden ball trick. I went back to my position and the pitcher caught on to what I was doing. He stayed close to the mound but didn't step on the rubber. [It's a balk if a pitcher steps on the rubber without the ball.] I just waited for Grich to lead off and then I tagged him. I heard he really got teased about it.

"What's really funny was that [Angels manager] Gene Mauch, who's a stickler for heads-up base running, said, 'You'll never see that play pulled off against us again.' Two weeks later, Doug DeCinces had doubled and I got the ball back in and I thought I'd try it again. I got him. Ever since then, Mauch has disliked me."

At first base, Dave Bergman takes an entirely different approach to hoodwinking the runner. "His favorite trick begins when the pitcher throws over to first to hold the runner," says teammate Kirk Gibson.

"Bergy pretends to throw the ball back to the pitcher, but instead he hides it in his glove. A cocky runner—there are some in the league—will hop off the bag as soon as the first baseman throws the ball to the pitcher. That's when Bergy gets him." One of Bergman's victims was Alan Wiggins of the Orioles. During a game in 1986, Bergman faked a throw back to the pitcher and then waited a few seconds for Wiggins to step off the bag before tagging him out.

DEKING THE DEKERS

Tracy Jones of the Reds likes to turn the tables on infielders who decoy runners.

"He'll slide into second and act like he's hurt," says Reds manager Pete Rose. "I'll go out there and ask, 'What's wrong?' He'll say, 'Nothing, I'm just decoying so I can steal third base.'"

WHICH PLAYERS ARE MOST ADEPT AT PULLING OFF THE "PHANTOM TAG"?

1. **Ozzie Smith**
2. **Tony Fernandez**
3. **Willie Randolph**
4. **Alfredo Griffin**
5. **Ryne Sandberg**
6. **Alan Trammell**

To make the typical double play, the shortstop or second baseman must have possession of the ball when he touches the bag before he throws over to first. But more often than you think, the infielder doesn't touch the bag, or if he does, it's without the ball. The feet can be quicker than the eye.

"The unwritten rule in the major leagues is that any time the ball beats a runner to a base and everything looks like it's been handled cleanly, then he's out," says Dan Plesac of the Brewers. "That's the way it should be. If you had to stand on second and make sure you had the ball before turning a double play, you would get your legs ripped apart by the runner's cleats."

Because infielders usually pull off the illegal phantom tag as a matter of survival, umpires rarely call them on it unless their deception becomes too obvious. "It's almost common practice that if the infielder is in the vicinity and he makes it look good, he'll get away with it," says Mets coach Bill Robinson.

According to the *Baseball Confidential* survey, the player most adept at the phantom tag is Cardinals shortstop Ozzie Smith. "Every shortstop in the league cheats a little at times," claims Braves second baseman Glenn Hubbard. "But Ozzie is the best." Adds one of Smith's admiring teammates, "Ozzie is so spectacular when he leaps across the bag that it'd be a crime to call it on him."

Willie Randolph of the Yankees has perfected the art of straddling the bag during his double-play pivot rather than touching the base with his foot. "He's been doing it for years that way and I swear he never tags the base," says Butch Wynegar of the Angels. "But he's always right around the bag so the umpires don't say anything."

Slick infielders such as Ryne Sandberg of the Cubs, Alfredo Griffin of the Athletics, Tony Fernandez of the Blue Jays, and Alan Trammell of the Tigers use the phantom tag to compensate for a bad toss or bad timing. "They make it look so smooth, they just glide right by the bag," says Bobby Meacham of the Yankees.

Sandberg and Fernandez also get high marks from their peers for another version of the phantom tag—tagging out the runner without touching him. Infielders employ this trick of the trade when the ball has easily beaten the runner. They simply bang their glove down in front of the bag and pull it up again without touching the runner—and without getting hurt.

"When Sandberg gets the ball, he hits the dirt with his glove and causes a big cloud of dust. Nobody can see if he actually tags the runner but the ump still calls him out," claims Hubie Brooks of the Expos. "I try to do it as much as I can, and I'm getting better at it."

Kent Tekulve of the Phillies defends the phantom tag, declaring that it's designed for the protection of the infielder. "Fans come out to see these stars play. It would be terrible to have a guy like Ozzie Smith on the DL because he got spiked on a play where the runner was obviously out. The phantom tag keeps the players out on the field and healthy."

The same rationale can't be made for a third kind of phantom tag—when the first baseman pulls his foot off the bag before the fielder's throw arrives. This is intended to make the umpire believe that the throw beat the runner to first. Among those considered the best at stealing a half a step from the runner are Eddie Murray of the Orioles and Keith Hernandez of the Mets.

 ## WHICH RUNNERS ARE BEST AT BREAKING UP THE DOUBLE PLAY?

1. **Bill Madlock**
2. **Kirk Gibson**
3. **Don Baylor**
4. **Lonnie Smith**
5. **George Brett**

In the old days of sharpened spikes and body rolls, mean, grizzled runners used the double-play ball as an excuse to blast into the pivot man at second and send him flying into the outfield.

But those days are gone. "I don't know of any guys who try to go into second to deliberately hurt someone," says Braves second baseman Glenn Hubbard. That's because players have too much to lose. "It's a different game today on the base paths," says Butch Wynegar of the Angels. "With the big contracts and all, players don't want to risk any unnecessary injuries going into second. They're willing to give themselves up at second if the game isn't on the line."

Even though the rolling block—the breakup artist's main weapon—has been outlawed, aggressive runners are still left with a few subtle techniques to thwart a twin killing.

Take, for example, Bill Madlock of the Tigers, whose tough base-running style has earned him the nickname "Mad Dog." "Madlock was great at throwing the rolling block," said an infielder who's been bloodied more than once by him. "But even though it has been eliminated, he's still dangerous. He has perfected the art of throwing the forearm clip. He clips you in the chest or the leg with his forearm as he slides into the bag."

Madlock's other technique—dumping the infielder by sliding as far off the base path as possible without getting called for interference—helped the Tigers win the AL East in 1987. In a crucial, late-season clash with the Blue Jays, Madlock slid hard into All-Star shortstop Tony Fernandez, who fractured his arm on the play. After seeing the replay, the Blue Jays claimed that Madlock had gone out of the base path when he slid into the shortstop. Fernandez was lost for the final nine games of the season as the Blue Jays slipped from first place and finished second to the Tigers.

The runners best at breaking up the DP aren't necessarily the fastest. Kirk Gibson of the Tigers has gained a reputation for taking out the pivot man. "Gibson is not dirty; he's intense," says Dan Plesac of the Brewers. "He goes in with the single-minded purpose of breaking up the double play. This year against our team, the Tigers had a runner on third and Gibson on first with one out. There was a grounder to short that looked like we'd get two and be out of the inning. But Gibson took out our second baseman Juan Castillo with an aggressive slide. The Tigers scored a run and kept the rally going because of Gibson's hard playing."

No one loves a shot at the pivot man more than Don Baylor of the Red Sox, says former teammate Steve Lyons of the White Sox. "He taught me that when you're a runner on first and there are less than two outs, your only job is to take out the infielder. When Baylor is on first, he almost hopes the batter behind him hits a double-play ball just so he has a chance to break it up."

Lonnie Smith of the Royals is known around the majors as a runner who slides hard and high. "He almost always gets a piece of you on the double play," says Hubie Brooks of the Expos. "He used to get me pretty good when he played for the Cardinals."

George Brett also gets plenty of praise from his peers for his ability to break up the double play with a charging, tough slide. But he's also come up with a unique approach. Recalls rookie Billy Ripkin of the Orioles, "I was starting a double play when Brett came running toward second screaming his head off. He was screaming as loud as he could. I thought the man was nuts."

 ## WHICH INFIELDERS SLAP THE HARDEST TAGS ON BASE RUNNERS?

1. **George Brett**
2. **Kent Hrbek**
3. **Bill Buckner**
4. **Jim Presley**
5. **Julio Franco**

First basemen seem to have a penchant for slapping hard tags on runners.

George Brett, who moved to first base after 14 years at third, quickly gained a reputation for his stinging tags. Explains Brett, "I'm new at the position so I tell everybody who gets to first base, 'Don't take a big lead off because every time the pitcher throws over here, I'm going to tag you harder. If you don't take a big lead off, then he won't throw over here as often.' The more the pitcher throws over here, the better chance I have of missing the pickoff throw myself. So I definitely tag hard."

Ray Knight of the Orioles knows painfully well that Brett isn't kidding. "The other night, I was on first when the catcher threw to George to pick me off. George whirled around and hit me full-steam right in the nose and now it's cut and swollen. That's the hardest tag I've ever felt," said the veteran.

Runners say they seldom forget the painful tags slapped on them by Twins first baseman Kent Hrbek. "He loves to slap the guy on the ankle—very hard," claims Ken Schrom of the Indians. "Fortunately, there aren't too many hard taggers like Herbie."

When Bill Buckner plays first, he uses a mean-looking H-web glove that can cause all kinds of pain for a runner. Explains former teammate Steve Lyons of the White Sox, "With an H-web glove, there's not a lot of leather in the webbing, just a couple of straps so the ball is exposed more. When the pitcher throws to first, Buck catches it in the webbing and then slaps the runner with it, so you're tagged with more ball and less leather. Buck is a hard-nosed kind of guy and if he doesn't like you or if he is having an 0-for day, you're going to get a hard slap tag. I like to see the reactions of players after he hits them with it. He's so tough that no one is going to jump up and pop him one."

Indians shortstop Julio Franco also rates among the hardest taggers. "He can hurt you," says Lloyd Moseby of the Blue Jays. "In fact, when he tags you, he knocks off your helmet—and your head. He makes sure to let you know you've been tagged."

At third base, Jim Presley of the Mariners has left his imprint on a few runners' faces. He and Rick Dempsey of the Indians got into a wrestling match during a game in 1987 after Presley applied a hard tag. Dempsey tried to dislodge the ball as he slid into third. "I'd have done the same thing," Presley said, "but I can't take that crap."

Almost all infielders and catchers in the survey concede that they have laid a hard tag on a runner occasionally just for the sport of it. "Last night I got a chance to get Kevin Seitzer [of the Royals]," said Orioles reserve catcher Floyd Rayford. "They always say if a runner is coming to the plate, make him pay up. When Seitzer tried to score, I gave him an elbow in the head. It was a nice, clean shot."

Jesse Barfield of the Blue Jays claims the hard taggers sometimes do lay a glove on him—but gently. "None tag me hard because they know if they did, I'd hit them with a left hook."

Fortunately for runners, the two hardest taggers over the past 10 years have recently retired—Angels second baseman Bobby Grich and shortstop Tim Foli, who spent most of his 16-year career in the National League. Even though they are out of baseball, they garnered more votes than any active player in the survey for the hardest taggers.

"As you slid into second, Grich would give you a knee, push you with his arm, throw you off balance, and slap a mean tag," recalls Bobby Meacham of the Yankees. "He'd try to make you timid about coming back the next time." Bill Madlock says that Foli played much like Grich. "He liked to put his knee in your head and then try to make you see stars with a slap to the head."

Then there was the Pirates' Willie Stargell. He wasn't a hard tagger but he would apply a stinging one to speedster Lou Brock just to irritate him, recalls Stargell's former teammate Kent Tekulve of the Phillies. "I knew, Willie knew, and Lou knew that when I was pitching, there was no way we could get Lou out at second. He could steal anytime he wanted. Just to have a little fun, I would repeatedly throw over to first whenever Lou got on. Willie would catch the ball and whack him right on the ankle even though Lou was already standing on the base. I kept throwing over there and Willie kept pounding Lou in the ankle. Lou would get all mad and Willie and I would just laugh. That's all we could do. We knew he was going to steal second anyway."

A REAL STINKER

Twins first baseman Kent Hrbek admits to this embarrassing story: "Not too long ago, Mike Easler [of the Yankees] was leading off first. I bent over, waiting for a possible pickoff throw from the pitcher, when I farted right in Easler's face," recalls Hrbek. "On the next pitch, Easler took his leadoff—while holding his nose."

 ## WHO ARE THE BIGGEST SHOWBOATS AFTER HITTING HOME RUNS?

1. **Dave Parker**
2. **Mel Hall**
3. **Ricky Henderson**
4. **Gary Carter**
5. **Jeffrey Leonard**
6. **Pedro Guerrero**

Nothing grates on a pitcher more than when a batter belts a long drive, stands at the plate to watch the ball sail into the seats for a home run, and then trots around the bases—very slowly. This is showboat hitting at its best. And no one does it better than Dave Parker of the Reds.

"Parker is the number-one showboat because when he hits it, he knows immediately if it's gone," says San Diego superstar Tony Gwynn. "He just stands there and watches it." Parker then does what he calls "The Thing"—his home-run trot. Instead of jogging up the baseline to first base, he takes a slow, extra wide turn in front of the first-base dugout. As he shuffles around the bases, he flicks his fingers in front of his chest.

"After Parker watches his homer, it's as if he goes into the dugout, gets a drink, changes his uniform, gives his teammates high-fives, and then rounds the bases," says the Mets' Roger McDowell. Adds Charlie Kerfeld of the Astros, "Dave Parker has the slowest trot of any human alive. A guy in a wheelchair could get around the bases faster." Kerfeld is not exaggerating. Parker holds the unofficial record for the longest home-run trot—31 seconds.

Mel Hall of the Indians is following in Parker's footsteps. On Easter Sunday in 1987, Hall took 28 seconds to circle the bases, according to Indians pitcher Tom Candiotti, who timed him. "He stood at the plate for about eight seconds. He wants to be timed every time he hits a home run. If he doesn't reach 30 seconds, he's disappointed." Hall used to carry three sets of batting gloves in his rear pockets. According to a teammate: "Mel told us it was to wave good-bye to the opposing players that he'd run past during his home-run trot." (League officials have ruled that players can only carry one set of gloves.)

Another showboat, Yankees outfielder Rickey Henderson, "annoys most of the pitchers," says Royals reliever Dan Quisenberry. Explains Rickey's teammate Bobby Meacham, "He drops the bat at the plate, throws his hands back, watches the ball until it disappears, and then begins a real slow jog toward first." Henderson is such a showboat that when he clouted a four-bagger against the University of Florida during a spring-training game in 1987, he danced around the bases. (Said Gator pitcher Jim McAndrew after the game, "If this had been a Southeastern Conference game and a guy did that, I'd deck him the next time up.")

Gary Carter of the Mets takes too much time after swatting a homer, says Cardinals manager Whitey Herzog. "He really loves to cheer over his homers even when his team is up by eight runs or down by eight." Several players in the *Baseball Confidential* survey said what antagonizes them the most are the frequent curtain calls Carter and the Mets take.

During the 1987 National League Championship Series, a nation-wide TV audience saw firsthand why players named Jeffrey Leonard of the Giants a home-run showboat. As soon as his first homer of the Series cleared the fence, Leonard came almost to a dead stop near second base and then took a slow trot around the bases. For another one of his round-trippers, Leonard did his "dead arm" trot—saunter-ing around the bases with his left arm held straight down by his side. "He can piss you off with his showboating," says a Reds player.

Dodgers outfielder Pedro Guerrero also likes to "dog it around the bases a little bit," said Tony Gwynn. Adds Charlie Kerfeld, "Guerrero's middle name is 'Dog.' " Cubs pitcher Rick Sutcliffe, who used to room with Guerrero, fumed when Pedro spent too long staring at a homer he hit off Sutcliffe at Wrigley Field in 1987. "The thing that gets me mad is that Pete and I used to be good friends in the minor leagues," said Sutcliffe. "For a friend to embarrass me like that, maybe I'd better reexamine just how good a friend he is."

Red Sox hitting star Wade Boggs doesn't believe in showboating at the plate. "You don't have to embarrass other players," he says. "We're such an elite group of athletes that you don't have to rub it in."

However, not all pitchers feel embarrassed by showboats. Says Orioles hurler Mike Boddicker, "If I'm going to give up a home run, I hope it's a good one and not a cheap one. I like watching the real long ones." Those sentiments are shared by Angels reliever Donnie Moore. "It doesn't bother me if a guy stands and watches the ball go into the seats. Hell, it's my fault for throwing it."

No batter dares showboat against Red Sox pitching ace Roger Clemens because, he says, "they know they have to come to the plate against me again."

WHO ARE THE GUTSIEST CATCHERS IN COLLISIONS AT HOME PLATE?

1. **Mike Scioscia**
2. **Rick Dempsey**
3. **Mike Heath**
4. **Lance Parrish**

Who's the best at blocking the plate? It's no contest. Players in both leagues rate Mike Scioscia of the Dodgers number one. "No one comes close," says Bill Madlock. "He's tough, he's Italian, and he's crazy." Manager Sparky Anderson claims, "You've got to take a jackhammer to move him." Adds Charlie Kerfeld of the Astros, "He has shown me some balls. He's the best. He gets smoked about five times a season—and he takes it."

To be more accurate, try five times a week. That's how often "Iron Mike" was involved in bone-jarring collisions at home during the first week of the 1986 season. Each time, he held on to the ball. In the season opener, Scioscia withstood a charge by Carmelo Martinez of the Padres. The next night, he held on against Marvell Wynne. Then Giants catcher Bob Brenly tried to bowl him over, followed later in that game by Candy Maldonado. Two days later, Chili Davis smashed into Scioscia—and the Giant left the game with a sprained shoulder.

No body-crunching collision at home is talked about more around the league than the crack-up Scioscia had with Jack Clark of the Cardinals in 1985. Scioscia held on to the ball and tagged out Clark, even though Mike was knocked out and had to be carried off on a stretcher. He was hospitalized overnight for a concussion, but, amazingly, he returned the next night to pinch-hit and catch in the ninth inning.

Scioscia's reputation for blocking the plate has given runners plenty to ponder on their dashes home. Tony Gwynn of the Padres confessed that while he was racing around third base with the winning run in a 1987 game, his mind was 90 feet down the line. "All I wanted to do was get there before the ball," he said. "I sure didn't want any part of Scioscia. I took him on once and paid the price." That happened two years earlier when Gwynn injured his wrist—which hurt for a month—after ramming into Scioscia.

Like Scioscia, Rick Dempsey of the Indians seems to relish contact at the plate. "In a game in 1985, Jim Presley [of the Mariners] was trying to score and Rick had him out by quite a bit," recalls Dempsey's former teammate, Cal Ripkin, Jr., of the Orioles. "Rick could have chosen to catch the ball and then tag him as he went by. But instead, Rick stayed in there, blocked the plate, and initiated the collision. It was a big collision. It seems like that gets him fired up. That puts some spark into the club when that happens." Adds Scott McGregor of the Orioles, "I don't know if Rick is gutsy or stupid. But he always gets the ball and just ducks his head and takes whatever is coming his way and gets blasted."

When Pirates coach Ray Miller was with the Orioles, he marveled at the way Dempsey stood his ground in two head-on collisions at home in the same inning. "He ran up the line and put his head down into the shoulder of each runner—and he did it without a helmet—and got them out. When the inning was over, he came into the dugout and Eddie Murray said, 'Gee, Rick, why didn't you keep your head up?' Rick had tears in his eyes from the pain and said, 'Hey, big boy. Why don't you take on one of those big bastards head-on before you tell me how to do it.' He's tough."

So tough he took on Royals part-time football player Bo Jackson in a fierce collision that belonged in an NFL highlights film. In a 1987 game, Jackson barreled into Dempsey with such force that Dempsey reeled eight feet backwards while his glove flew off in one direction and his mask in another. Yet he managed to hang on to the ball, which he had shifted to his bare hand, and tagged Jackson out. However, Dempsey suffered a dislocated and cracked left thumb and went on the disabled list.

Two other catchers most prominently mentioned for their courage are also graduates of the old school of no-guts-no-glory backstoppers—the Tigers' Mike Heath and the Phillies' Lance Parrish, who put in 10 years of service in Detroit.

"If Mike has the ball before you get there, you're history," says teammate Dave Bergman. "He'll do anything in the world to keep you from getting to home plate." Heath has something else going for him besides guts, says the Angels' Butch Wynegar. "He's got that high-strung personality that makes him adamant—he's not going to let you in, period."

About Lance Parrish, Sparky Anderson says runners have learned a simple lesson: "If you try to run into Lance, you're just going to get yourself hurt." Lloyd Moseby of the Blue Jays says National Leaguers are discovering what American League base runners already know: "Lance stands right in there and takes everything you have to give him. I'm glad he's out of this league, believe me."

Most other catchers avoid collisions by using the sweep tag. They creep up on the infield side of the plate and then try to tag the runner as he goes by. This technique cuts down on injuries. Catcher Terry Kennedy of the Orioles questions whether backstoppers such as Scioscia and Dempsey should instigate collisions when it's not necessary. "I think most catchers will hang in there and block the plate when they have to. It depends upon how important the run is." Wynegar concurs, adding, "If it's the tying or winning run, then you sacrifice everything you've got. You roll with the blow. Unless you're Scioscia, Dempsey, Heath, or Parrish—then you let the runner bounce off of you."

▲

A BIG DUMMY AT THE PLATE

After tagging out the Royals' Danny Tartabull in a collision at home in 1987, Athletics catcher Terry Steinbach credited a football drill for preparing him.

In the drill, practiced during spring training, Steinbach caught throws to the plate while coach Rene Lachemann kept tossing a wide football tackling dummy at him. "You'd have to catch the ball and make the tag the same time as he threw the dummy at you," Steinbach explained. "I thought, 'What the hell kind of drill is this?' But it's paid off."

HOW RUNNERS STEAL CATCHERS' SIGNS

Crafty base runners do more than steal bases. They sometimes steal signs. Perched on second base, a runner enjoys a perfect vantage point to see and study the opposing catcher's signs. And once he figures them out, he can secretly relay them to the batter.

"Many second basemen and shortstops know how to steal the catcher's signs," says the Cubs' All-Star second sacker Ryne Sandberg, considered among the best sign-stealing runners in the league. "We're used to catcher's signs because when we're out in the field, we see the signs that our own catcher is giving our pitcher.

"There aren't that many different ways for catchers to give signs. So when I'm a base runner on second, I study the opposing catcher. Once I catch on to his routine, I signal to my teammate at the plate."

The runner-to-batter signals are usually verbal such as shouting out names or code words. Ozzie Smith of the Cardinals says that Pedro Guerrero and Mariano Duncan and other Spanish-speaking Dodgers will holler code words in their native tongue. "Sometimes if you're batting and the runner calls you by your first name, a fastball is coming and if he calls you by your last name, a curveball is coming," Smith explained. "Personally, I don't like that kind of information. It's more important for the batter to know the location of the pitch than the type of pitch."

Cubs runners usually flash the location of the pitch, says Sandberg. "If the runner signals inside, then I know it's probably going to be a fastball because it's hard to throw a good breaking ball that will end up inside."

However, many batters say they're not interested in receiving stolen signs because it disrupts their concentration. "We've got enough to think about up there," contends Bill Almon of the Mets. "Besides, the batter can get hurt. What if you're wrong? You might signal to him that the pitch will be a curve on the outside part of the plate, so he leans in for the breaking ball and the pitcher throws one inside. If the catcher thinks his signs are being stolen, he may signal for a curve outside but that really might mean a fastball inside. All in all, it's safer to be on my own up there."

ON THE FIELD

PLAYING WITH PAIN

Unless he's as lucky as a pitcher with a 10-run lead, the everyday player is plagued by nagging aches and injuries. But he must play through the pain if he wants to stay in the lineup. There's an old saying in baseball: "If your injury isn't enough to stop your career, then you better be playing."

Players get hurt in more ways than they can score runs: fouling a ball off the foot, colliding with a teammate, taking a fastball on the wrist, getting spiked. Hidden underneath uniforms are purple bruises the size of lemons and more tape than a museum full of mummies.

"I don't think there's a player today who has felt 100 percent healthy every day for a whole season," says Mike Flanagan of the Orioles. "You're lucky if you feel 100 percent half the time." Adds Rick Rhoden of the Yankees, "We all suffer aches and pains. Some guys tolerate pain better than others, but if you want to be a big leaguer, you have to play with pain."

Those who play in pain are called gamers. Here's a sampling from the *Baseball Confidential* survey of what being a gamer is all about:

Pete Incaviglia, Rangers: "Incaviglia has played through pain and injury throughout the 1987 season," says his manager, Bobby Valentine. "He got hit on the elbow and it swelled up three times its size. It was still swollen two months later. He doesn't care about pain."

Cal Ripkin, Jr., Orioles: "There are times when he gets hit by a pitch and can't bend his arm or his leg," says Buddy Biancalana of the Royals. "He just works it off. He's got guys coming in trying to spike him, kick him, and bowl him over. You know he gets hurt, but he's out there every inning. To play 8,000-plus consecutive innings is incredible."

Keith Hernandez, Mets: "I've seen him in the clubhouse with a 103-degree temperature throwing up and then just lay there until game time," says former teammate Ed Lynch of the Cubs. "Then he'll go out and play as hard as ever. Afterward, he looks like he's ready to pass out."

Kirk Gibson, Tigers: "Talk about a tough gamer," says former teammate Bill Scherrer of the Reds. "In 1985, he was hit by a pitch square in the jaw. He spit blood out and then jogged to first base. They almost had to drag him off the field to get him to the hospital for an examination."

Tim Flannery, Padres: "The man just doesn't think about broken bones, bruises, and cuts," says teammate Tony Gwynn. "With some guys, you sprain your pinky and you're out for a week. With Flan, he was playing with busted ribs for a week. You can't imagine how painful it is to swing a bat with busted ribs. But that's Flan. He goes all out whether he's hurt or not." Adds former teammate Jerry Royster of the White Sox, "If Tim isn't bleeding by the end of the game, then he feels he hasn't played hard enough."

Johnny Ray, Pirates: "In 1986, Johnny was batting nearly .400 when he pulled a groin muscle real bad," says former teammate Bill Almon of the Mets. "Despite the pain, he played because he knew how badly the team needed him. His performance fell off because of the injury, but the team would have been worse off without him. Even though he should have been on the DL for a few weeks, he stayed in the lineup for the good of the team and still batted .300."

Bo Diaz, Reds: "I've seen his knees," says former teammate Mike LaValliere of the Pirates. "They're scarred and swollen and every time he squats to catch, it makes me hurt just watching him. I have healthy knees and they hurt after a game so I can imagine how his feel."

Bill Buckner, Red Sox: "Many players wouldn't go through what he has to do every day," says teammate Rich Gedman. "For years, he's played on very painful ankles. He has to put DMSO [a medication] on them, ice them down, tape them up, give them heat, and rub them. It takes more than an hour every day for him just to get his ankles ready. He's truly amazing. I mean, that's dedication."

A REAL BRUISER

Brian Downing of the Angels enjoys showing off his bruises as if they were badges of honor.

"When he gets hit by a pitch, which happens to him more than anyone else on this team, he likes to show the bruise to us," says teammate Butch Wynegar. "Whenever he gets a welt that is all swollen and black and blue, he's proud of it. He goes around to us and says, 'Hey, look at this one. Yeah, it's sure pretty, isn't it?' "

GAMERS

Ron Oester, Reds—The second baseman, who hates to make excuses as much as he hates to complain, played most of the 1986 season in terrible pain. But he kept his suffering from his teammates. Not until spring training of 1987 was the truth revealed. An arthrogram on his left shoulder revealed a torn muscle, and X rays of his left ankle showed that two bones had been broken.

Ed Correa, Rangers—Ignoring pain, the starting pitcher hurled 90 m.p.h. fastballs for 10 games during the 1987 season with a fractured shoulder blade.

Jody Davis, Cubs—On Opening Day of the 1987 season, the catcher broke a finger on his throwing hand. Despite the injury, he kept playing and then suffered a broken toe. Still, he remained in the lineup.

Dale Murphy, Braves—In 1986, he cut his right hand on the fence after catching a fly ball and required nine stitches to close the wound. Although the Braves announced he would be out for a week, Murphy—his injured hand bandaged up—appeared as a pinch hitter the next night and blasted a homer.

Eric Davis, Reds—Even though he had a pulled groin muscle that required icing before and after games, Davis stole three bases and leaped above the wall to take a home run away from Darryl Strawberry in a 1987 game. The year before, he belted a homer to enter the exclusive "20-60 Club" (20 homers and 60 stolen bases in one season) while wearing a flak jacket and body wrap around bruised ribs and tape around a sore left wrist.

Andre Dawson, Cubs—The 1987 National League MVP suffers chronic pain from bad, swollen knees. When he played for the Expos, Dawson spent nearly two hours before game time having his knees treated and wrapped. Three or four times a year, his knees had to be drained.

▲

PLAYERS WHO ALWAYS COMPLAIN ABOUT THEIR ACHES AND PAINS

1. Rickey Henderson
2. Chris Brown
3. Leon Durham
4. Mike Marshall

▲

IT ONLY HURTS WHEN YOU LAUGH

Some injuries hurt the ego as well as the body. Here are some of the strangest injuries that players have recently talked about—and, in most cases, chuckled over—in clubhouses around the league:

Greg Harris, Rangers—The righthanded pitcher missed two starts in 1987 because of "sunflower-seed elbow." During a game between starts, Harris was flicking sunflower seeds from the dugout to a friend in the stands. A few hours later, Harris's right elbow began to swell and he discovered he couldn't throw without experiencing pain. "I know," Harris said sheepishly. "It sounds ridiculous."

Ron Kittle, Yankees—He went on the 15-day disabled list in 1987 after he pulled a neck muscle while toting a stretcher for injured teammate Lenn Sakata. Kittle's neck sustained another weird injury a few years earlier. "I sneezed so hard that I hurt my neck and had to miss a game," he said.

Manny Trillo, Cubs—Minutes before he was to start in a 1987 game, Trillo trimmed the nail on his big toe too closely. When he put on his shoes, his toe became too irritated for him to play and he was scratched from the lineup.

Marvell Wynne, Padres—Wynne was simply stepping away in the batter's box from a fourth ball when he suffered severe back spasms in a 1987 game. Wynne, who was taken to the hospital on a stretcher, was placed on the 15-day disabled list, prompting trainer Dick Dent to say, "This may be the first time in baseball history that a guy has had to go to the hospital after drawing a walk."

Glenn Braggs, Brewers: "We were going through customs in Toronto, and when he placed his luggage on the conveyor belt, he stubbed his toe," said teammate Rick Manning. The injury put Braggs out of action for a whole week in 1987. "That's one strange injury," said Manning.

Oddibe McDowell, Rangers—At a banquet early in the 1987 season, McDowell was trying to butter a roll when he sliced open his right middle finger with a butter knife. He was out for two weeks.

John Tudor, Cardinals—Tudor was injured while sitting in the dugout in 1987. Mets catcher Barry Lyons was chasing a pop foul when he slid right into the Cardinals' dugout and crashed into Tudor. Tudor, who suffered a broken bone just below the knee, was out for more than three months. (The pop foul landed several rows into the seats behind the dugout.)

Alan Trammell, Tigers—He was dressed up as Frankenstein for a Halloween party. The scary thing for him was that he tripped, damaged his knee, and wound up needing surgery.

Charlie Hough, Rangers—The veteran hurler suffered a broken little finger on his pitching hand in 1986 from shaking hands. Hough, who was out for a month, injured his hand when he and a friend engaged in a semi-high-five.

Wade Boggs, Red Sox—Boggs was putting on his cowboy boots in his hotel room when he lost his balance and fell, banging his ribs on the arm of a couch. His ribs were so sore he missed a week of action in 1986.

Glenn Wilson, Phillies—He was sidelined for several days in 1986 by, of all things, a baby's crib. Wilson cut his foot while assembling the crib.

Kirk Gibson, Tigers—He missed two games in 1986 after his dog bit him on the hand in a fight with a neighbor's dog.

Vince Coleman, Cardinals—Shortly before the 1985 World Series, Coleman was loosening up at practice when he was literally run over by the automatic tarpaulin machine. His leg injury was so serious that he missed the entire Series.

Brett Butler, Indians—From the bullpen, teammate Bryan Clark heaved a ball toward Butler for outfield warm-ups before the eighth inning of a 1985 game. Butler didn't see the ball coming and it struck his elbow, knocking him out of the game.

Wayne Gross, Orioles—As he raced to cover third on an attempted steal, Gross's sunglasses slipped off his nose. Just then, catcher Rick Dempsey's throw struck him between the eyes. Gross, who needed three stitches to close the wound, said at the time, "You're supposed to have your glove up in that situation. But I figured if I got hit in the chest, I'd have been killed. It hit me in the forehead, so I'm okay." Despite his bull's-eye throw, Dempsey was charged with the error. "I hate to beg for an error," said Gross, "but that one was mine."

WHAT A CUT-UP

When Ed Whitson pitched for the Padres in 1984, he turned an injury into an opportunity.

"The night before he was scheduled to pitch against the Phillies, he was fooling around with a pop-top can and cut his finger," recalls former teammate Gary Lucas of the Angels. "Ed couldn't grip the ball the right way for a curve or a change-up. So he came up with a palm ball—and threw a two-hit shutout."

THE "I GUYS" vs. TEAM PLAYERS

On one end of the 24-man roster are the consummate team players who go above and beyond the call of duty for the good of the club. On the other side are the "I Guys" who care more about their personal performance than the team's.

Most every team has at least one player on each end of the spectrum, according to the *Baseball Confidential* survey.

"There are quite a few guys in the league who are more concerned about their own stats than winning or losing," says Rick Manning of the Brewers. "Believe me, you can see it. When the team wins and they don't get any hits, they sit by their lockers and sulk. And when the team loses and they get three or four knocks, they're as cheerful as can be."

It happens on pennant winners as well as cellar dwellers, although more often on losers, says Jerry Reed of the Mariners. "Take, for instance, 1985 when I was with Cleveland and we lost 102 games. The team was doing terrible. Toward the end of the year in a situation like that, you have to care about how you're doing personally. When you go in to negotiate your contract for the next year, you aren't negotiating on how the team did; it's how you did. There's a fine line between helping the team and helping yourself."

Fortunately, clubs are stocked with players who believe in the popular locker-room slogan: "There is no 'I' in team." Of these team players, a few stand out in the eyes of their peers for their willingness to make sacrifices for the good of the team.

Don Mattingly, Yankees—In 1986, when injuries left the Yankees without a third baseman for a few days, the Gold Glove first baseman stepped forward to play three games at the hot corner—even though he is lefthanded. "No one would have given it a second thought had he not volunteered," said a teammate. "But he risked embarrassment to himself and possible injury by playing an unfamiliar position just to help out the team. He did extremely well too." Mattingly is believed to be only the 28th southpaw in major league history to play third base. Lefties traditionally don't play third because they must twist their bodies to make the necessary throws across the infield.

Greg Gross, Phillies—Even though he owns a career batting average of over .290, Gross is seldom in the starting lineup. "He's one of the game's best pinch hitters, and because of that, it's doomed him to a role on the bench," says a teammate. "There are times when he's frustrated about it, but it hasn't affected his performance. He has accepted his role as a player who can come off the bench and deliver. All he really cares about is helping the team to win."

Tim Flannery, Padres: "Tim will sacrifice his body to get on base," says former teammate Jerry Royster of the White Sox. "I played with him for two years in 1985 and 1986, and in crucial situations, he must have been hit by a pitch at least four times. One time, when we were trailing by a run in the ninth inning and Tim was leading off, he got hit by a John Denny pitch that was only three inches off the plate inside. Denny was furious. If it's a tight game and Flannery is leading off, the pitcher better find some way to pitch him away because if it's anywhere in sight, Tim is going to get hit."

Dave Bergman, Tigers: "He's a great example of how to be a not-everyday player," says teammate Kirk Gibson. "He's a student of the game, and when he's on the bench, he helps the manager, looking to steal signs or spot something in the opposing pitcher's delivery. He's ready to play at a moment's notice and is always prepared. He's totally into the game."

WHICH OUTFIELDERS PLAY WITH THE MOST RECKLESS ABANDON?

1. **Len Dykstra**
2. **Gary Pettis**
3. **Chet Lemon**
4. **Brian Downing**
5. **Fred Lynn**

They are the wallbangers, the tough-as-nails outfielders who won't let a mere fence slow them down in their all-out pursuit of a deep drive.

Mets centerfielder Len Dykstra is not afraid to challenge a wall, says Terry Kennedy of the Orioles. "He's always crashing into the walls. One time he dove for a ball on the warning track while running full speed. He slid and hit his head on the wall and knocked himself out." The play resulted in an inside-the-park homer for Glenn Davis of the Astros in 1985. Even so, says a Houston player, Dykstra "is still a kamikaze." Adds Mets coach Bill Robinson, "There are some ball parks like Wrigley Field where you'd be crazy to dive into the wall because behind those vines are a whole lot of bricks—yet Dykstra will dive into them if he has to."

There's a fine line between reckless abandon and aggressiveness, says Mike Easler of the Yankees. "Lenny nearly broke his neck on one play because he may have been too reckless. But that's only because he thinks he can catch anything in the ball park and he goes all out."

Centerfielder Gary Pettis and left fielder Brian Downing, both of the Angels, won't let a wall stop them. In fact, they practice banging into fences. Coach Jimmie Reese "tries to hit us balls as close to the wall as possible," says Pettis. "I try to measure my steps from the warning track to the fence so I can prepare for the crash." Shortly after suffering two collisions with Downing in left center in 1986, Pettis slammed into the wall at Arlington Stadium to make a catch. "I'd rather hit the wall than Brian Downing, that's for sure," said Pettis.

Downing has "no regard for his body," claims a former teammate. "That's just the way he plays the game. He hurts himself out there, but he plays every day." Downing accepts the pain, says Los Angeles beat writer Peter Schmuck. "Many times I've seen him with large purplish-blue welts on his body from crashing into a fence or hitting a railing. He cares little about his own personal safety."

Chet Lemon of the Tigers knows only one way to play—with total abandon. "For years, he's destroyed himself out there," says Scott McGregor of the Orioles. "It doesn't matter if it's a close game or not, he'll dive after balls and crash into walls." Blue Jays star Lloyd Moseby says that with the number of times Lemon slams into fences, "You'd think he'd hustle himself right out of baseball." Some of the Brewers still talk about the 1987 game in Detroit when Lemon robbed B. J. Surhoff of an extra-base hit, says Dan Plesac of the Brewers. "Lemon ran full speed right into the steel wall at Tiger Stadium and made the catch. It was a tough, gutsy play—typical of Lemon."

Like other wallbangers, Fred Lynn of the Orioles won't be fenced in. In 1985, manager Earl Weaver told Lynn to be more careful because the team couldn't afford to lose him to injury. But Lynn has kept crashing into walls anyway, bending several outfield fence posts. This prompted Memorial Stadium groundskeeper Pat Santarone to declare, "Lynn doesn't even know the wall is there. You should see it. There are four or five bent poles. He's going to knock the wall down someday." Teammate Floyd Rayford says that Lynn has plastered himself against fences so many times that the team is used to it. "We peel him off the fence and bring him back in. All he says is, 'Just going hard. Just going hard.'"

Here are some comments about two other fearless players:

Mel Hall, Indians: "He's constantly running into fences and he seems to get a thrill out of it," says Cleveland beat writer Mike Peticca. "Mel says that he's a gunfighter and a gunfighter never backs down."

Rob Deer, Brewers: "I saw Rob crash into a fence so hard that when he came back into the dugout, he had part of the fence imprinted on his face," says former teammate Mark Grant of the Padres.

PLAYERS WHO MAKE EASY CATCHES LOOK HARD

1. Rickey Henderson
2. Len Dykstra
3. Dave Parker
4. Gary Matthews
5. Mel Hall

WHAT DO PLAYERS ON THE FIELD THINK ABOUT BESIDES BASEBALL?

Even though they should be focusing their undivided attention on the game, players admit they sometimes daydream out on the field.

"Throughout a 162-game schedule, you can't concentrate on every pitch—it's impossible," says George Brett of the Royals. "One of my problems when I played third base was that it was so hard to concentrate every second of every inning of every game. I'd think about what happened on my last at-bat or my next at-bat and somebody would hit a ground ball to me and I wouldn't be ready. Once in New York, I was waving to some friends of mine in the front row and some guy hit me in the chest with a ground ball. Some players can concentrate 99 percent of the time; others only 70 percent. I was about 70 percent at third; now it's 99 percent for me at first."

Bill Madlock of the Tigers admits that he showed better concentration earlier in his career than he does now. "It seems the older you get, the more your mind wanders." What does he think about on the field other than baseball? "Sex," he declares. "I want to get as much as I can before I die. I think more about getting 3,000 conquests than 3,000 hits—because I know I'm never going to get 3,000 hits."

Here's a sampling of what other players think about on the field:

Mark Grant, Padres: "I think about how stupid some fans are that they'd actually sacrifice their lives to get a baseball. I've seen people dive over stadium chairs and crash into people just for a stupid baseball. I think about how those grown men try to steal a ball away from a little kid. On a serious note, I also like to check out the beef in the stands."

Jesse Barfield, Blue Jays: "What my wife is cooking for dinner."

Terry Kennedy, Orioles: "I think about a beach somewhere exotic like Tahiti where I'm laying in the sun, reading a book, and escaping for a little while."

Roger McDowell, Mets: "Whether my wife got to the game safely—especially here in New York."

Dave Bergman, Tigers: "How the fish are biting. I just picture myself on a boat and get myself in a tranquil mood."

Charlie Kerfeld, Astros: "Rock 'n' roll, girls, sex, and money."

Ray Knight, Orioles: "I try to concentrate totally on the game but sometimes my mind wanders, and most of the time when it does, I'm thinking about my family."

Hubie Books, Expos: "What I'm going to eat that night."

Lloyd Moseby, Blue Jays: "I'm singing to myself. I love the Temptations—they're one of the greatest groups of all times—and I sing their songs."

Mark Gubicza, Royals: "Every once in a while when it's not going too good for me on the mound, I look up in the stands to see how Lisa [his wife] is reacting. I look up there for support."

Bryn Smith, Expos: "Where I'd like to be other than right here in the ball park—golf courses, fishing holes, maybe a summer at home for a change."

WHO ARE THE SMARTEST DEFENSIVE PLAYERS IN BASEBALL?

1. **Cal Ripkin, Jr.**
2. **Marty Barrett**
3. **Ozzie Smith**
4. **Alan Trammell**

There may be flashier, quicker shortstops than the Orioles' Cal Ripkin, Jr., but none are smarter on the field, according to the *Baseball Confidential* survey.

"Cal doesn't have great range or a great arm, yet he gets the job done because he's smart," says Tim Laudner of the Twins. "I've never seen him out of position. He's always at the right place at the right time." Adds Scott Bailes of the Indians, "Ripkin isn't blessed with real quick foot speed, but he reacts quickly and plays every hitter differently. He adjusts to each pitch being thrown. He's such an intelligent player." Says fellow shortstop Ozzie Guillen of the White Sox, "Ripkin knows where everybody hits the ball. He's a machine. I've seen balls hit in the hole and he's positioned right there. He never has to move."

To cut down on the territory he has to cover, Ripkin says he takes educated gambles. "I study the other team's hitters and my pitchers carefully. If you work at it enough, over a period of time, you can have a pretty good idea which hitter is going to hit the ball to which spot on certain pitches. That's my only secret. I rely on probability."

Although Ripkin is rated as number one for defensive smarts, the shortstop he respects most is Alan Trammell of the Tigers. "He does everything the way it's supposed to be done. If you were teaching kids at a clinic, you'd show them Alan Trammell. He does everything textbook correct."

Trammell taught Tigers third baseman Darnell Coles a lesson during a game against the Rangers in 1987. "Tram wanted me to play back and the manager wanted me to play in," recalled Coles, now with the Pirates. "Scott Fletcher was up and Tram told me, 'He's going to hit a grounder in the hole between you and me, so back up three steps.' I didn't. Sure enough Fletcher hit it right where Tram said he would for a single. If I'd gone back three steps, I'd have gotten it."

An infielder who makes up in smarts what he lacks in natural talent is Marty Barrett of the Red Sox. "He always seems to do the right thing defensively," says Bill Schroeder of the Brewers. "When I'm thinking of heads-up players, I'm thinking of him." Barrett is more than a glove man out on the field, say his teammates. "He'll tell his pitcher if they're giving away [telegraphing] their pitches," says Rich Gedman. "He'll put a play on a runner if he sees him leaning just a bit. He'll talk to the pitcher about the little things that you need to help a ball club win." Even though Roger Clemens is a Cy Young Award winner, he still summons Barrett to the mound for advice. "There are times when I call Marty over and ask, 'What should I do here?' He knows the batters so well that he'll call a pitch. Then I go strike out the hitter and Marty feels like he threw the pitch."

In the National League, Ozzie Smith of the Cardinals is in a class by himself. Talking about the first $2 million glove man, Tony Gwynn of the Padres says, "Ozzie hardly ever makes a mistake. He has this sixth sense—he just knows where to go before the batter hits it and he's right there. And what agility. I saw Ozzie go up the middle after a ground ball. It took a bad hop and he bare-handed it, rolled over, got up, and threw a seed to first to get the runner."

Smith acts like a field general, positioning the whole infield. "A lot of communication goes on out there," he explains. "If I plan to move, I tell my third baseman. But since you can give away what pitch is coming by the way you position yourself, you wait until the last moment. Sometimes you can actually intimidate the hitter into doing certain things. For instance, if you go over into the hole, he might think a curveball is coming when really it's a fastball."

According to the survey, other players who possess exceptional defensive smarts are: Don Mattingly of the Yankees, Eddie Murray of the Orioles, Dwight Evans of the Red Sox, Mike Schmidt of the Phillies, Bill Doran of the Astros, Robin Yount of the Brewers, Gary Carter of the Mets, Alfredo Griffin of the Athletics, Willie Randolph of the Yankees, Dale Murphy of the Braves, Keith Hernandez of the

Mets, Kirby Puckett of the Twins, Tommy Herr of the Cardinals, and Ryne Sandberg of the Cubs.

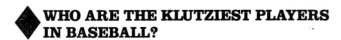

WHO ARE THE KLUTZIEST PLAYERS IN BASEBALL?

1. Lonnie Smith
2. Glenn Wilson

Some major leaguers play with such boundless energy and desire that their feet just can't keep up with the rest of their body. As a result, they spend more time in the dirt and grass than a ground hog. For pure klutziness on the field, no one can match Lonnie "Skates" Smith of the Royals and Glenn Wilson of the Phillies, according to the *Baseball Confidential* survey.

Smith has been tripping over his feet ever since he broke into the bigs in 1978. "When I hit the ball to the outfield and Lonnie starts running, he falls down all the time," says Ozzie Guillen of the White Sox. "Whenever I see Lonnie, he's always in the grass. He looks like he's on roller skates but doesn't know how to roller skate. That's why he has the nickname 'Skates.'"

A Twins player says that a Smith spill in the outfield grass once led to a 2–1 Royals defeat. "We were tied 1–1 in the ninth and had a runner on first. A Twin hit a drive down the left-field line and Lonnie fell and the winning run scored. It seems that Lonnie can't play a whole game without falling down somewhere, whether in the outfield or on the base paths. Every time we play the Royals we wonder how long it will be before Lonnie takes a dive." Says Smith's teammate George Brett, "We're going to have to sharpen Lonnie's spikes so he doesn't fall down."

Although Smith's peer in the National League, Glenn Wilson, has four fewer years' experience, he's giving Smith a stumbling run for his money. "Glenn goes at such a high level that sometimes he gets out of control and trips and falls all over the place," says teammate Von Hayes. "But he sure is fun to watch." Adds the Phils' Don

Carman, "Wilson falls down running around third base. He falls down in the outfield. He falls down making throws. He falls down swinging hard. I've even seen him accidentally hit himself in the head with the bat while in the batter's box."

Among other players named in the klutziest category are:

Alan Trammell, Tigers: "It's strange that a Gold Glove short-stop could be so klutzy, but he is—off the field," says a member of the team. "When he goes out to dinner, there's a good chance he'll have to have his shirt laundered afterward." Adds former teammate Darnell Coles of the Pirates, "Tram is always dropping something, spilling something. Once, just before he went on national TV for an interview, he spilled coffee all over himself."

George Frazier, Twins: "I'm always splitting my head open on the dugout roof or someplace. One year when I played for New York, I hit my head so many times that the Yankees called me 'Lumpy.' Graig Nettles and Goose Gossage even gave me a big silver belt buckle with the name 'Lumpy' on it."

Pete Incaviglia, Rangers: "He turns fielding into an exercise in futility," says a player. "He circles around a fly ball and makes managers hold their breath, wondering if he's going to stay on his feet—let alone catch it."

Rob Deer, Brewers: "Rob is a good athlete, but he seems to spend an awful lot of time on the ground," says teammate Rick Manning. "He's not usually clumsy, but it seems that when he rounds a base real quick, the next thing you know he's on the ground and crawling back to the base."

PLAYERS OPPOSING TEAMS LOVE TO HATE

1. Rickey Henderson
2. Gary Carter
3. George Bell
4. Pedro Guerrero
5. Reggie Jackson

WHAT SUPERSTITIONS DO
PLAYERS HAVE?

In no other sport are athletes as superstitious as they are in baseball. "I don't know what it is about this game," says Pete Incaviglia of the Rangers, "but baseball and superstition go hand in hand." Cy Young Award winner Roger Clemens—who, whenever he gets a new pair of sanitaries, wears them inside out for good luck—flatly declares, "If a player tells me he's not superstitious, he's lying."

Almost all players have a superstitious quirk. They engage in some little ritual, a secret habit, a certain way of dressing—all designed to bring them good luck. Here's a sampling of major league superstitions:

Rob Murphy, Reds: "I'll never take the ball from anyone between innings. Even if the umpire has it, I'll make him throw it on the ground. I also have a little ritual with the resin bag. I always dust my hand the same way. I dust my fingers first, my palm next, then the back of my hand, and my fingers again."

Wade Boggs, Red Sox—When he steps to the plate, he makes the sign of the Hebrew letter "chai," which stands for life.

Jerry Royster, White Sox: "If I'm starting, I run out to the mound after the national anthem and pick up the resin bag. I tap it twice in my glove and throw it over my right shoulder before I go out to my position. I've done that ever since I've been in the minors. Sometimes if the resin bag isn't on the mound when I arrive, I'll stay there until someone brings it out."

Dave Righetti, Yankees: "When he gets out of the car before the game, he taps the rearview mirror with his left hand," says teammate Ron Kittle.

Mike Schmidt, Phillies: "In 1986, Schmitty and the Phils were on a hot streak that started when he stopped at a WaWa [a local convenience store]," recalls Philadelphia beat writer Bill Brown. "I bumped into him at a WaWa during the middle of this streak and asked him what he was doing there. He said, 'I've been hitting and the team's been winning ever since I first came in here for a soda. So now I stop in here every day and buy a soda on my way to the park.' That's pretty rich for a guy who's headed for the Hall of Fame."

Baltimore Orioles: "When we were trying to stop a rally by another team, some of the guys in the dugout would roll up a towel real tight," says former Oriole Lenn Sakata of the Yankees. "They'd wait until Earl [Weaver] wasn't looking and then fire the towel right at [trainer] Ralph Salvon's head. It was done to bring us good luck. Another way was to hit him lightly in the shins with a bat."

Kirby Puckett, Twins: "I keep changing clothes trying to find something that will bring me luck. One time I put on new stirrups and hit a home run. But they got lost after the game. When I wore old stirrups the next day, we lost."

Dennis Martinez, Expos: "I only wear my hat when I pitch. Otherwise it stays off my head."

Joe Niekro, Twins: "Joe never takes his hat off," says former teammate Bill Dawley of the Cardinals. "During the national anthem, he goes in the tunnel so he can keep his hat on. When he batted [in the National League], he wore his cap under his batting helmet."

Kevin Seitzer, Royals: "I won't wash my stirrup socks until I take an 0-for. Then I'll throw them in the laundry."

Chris Bosio, Brewers: "When we began the [1987] season with 13 straight wins," says teammate Rick Manning, "Boz wore the same shorts every day without washing them."

Moose Haas, Athletics: "At the start of the 1986 season, my pants were a little big so I wore Dwayne Murphy's pants. I won six straight games. I tried rationalizing this good fortune and my superstitions. I never step on a foul line and I always put on my right shoe first, and I've been doing those for a long time. So it had to be Murphy's pants."

Gary Lucas, Angels: "I've worn Adidas shoes my whole career, but in 1987 I decided to switch to Nike. I began the season with an ERA of 12 something so I went back to Adidas and gave up only two runs in the next 15 innings."

Sammy Stewart, Indians: "If we're up to bat and we need a hit, I'll stamp my foot on the bench the same number of times that matches the number of the batter."

Gene Mauch, Angels manager: "The area in front of the dugout where Gene sits must be completely clean," says team trainer Rick Smith. "There can't be any sunflower seeds, gum wrappers, or Dixie cups. They have to be out of his sight."

Bill Wilkinson, Mariners—The Mariners reliever went through a closetful of baseball shoes in 1987. Each time he had what he considered a bad outing, he threw his cleats in a trash can. He deep-sixed six pairs that season.

REACH OUT AND TOUCH SOMEONE— BUT NOT KEITH RHOMBERG

The most superstitious player ever to set foot on a diamond in the 1980s was Keith Rhomberg, a reserve outfielder for the Indians from 1982–84.

"He wouldn't let anyone touch him last," said Milt Thompson of the Phillies, who played against him in winter ball. "If you touched him, he'd touch you back. One time, I took a baseball and touched him with it and then threw it over the fence. He went out there and tried to find it. Sometimes his teammates would gang up on him and they'd all touch him at the same time and then run. He'd go crazy trying to touch them all back."

It seemed like half the American League tried to touch him, said former teammate Rick Manning of the Brewers. "Then fans got in on the act. They sent Rhomberg letters saying, 'You touched my letter— I got you last.' So he'd write them back just so he could be last."

Rhomberg had some other superstitions as well, said Manning. "He would never put his helmet on while in the on-deck circle. He'd leave it on the ground and point it toward the pitcher. Also, he would never make a right turn. If he approached the batter's box from the right side, he'd walk in front of the plate and make a left to the batter's box. If he made an out at first, he'd always turn left 270 degrees before going into the first-base dugout. He was by far the most superstitious player I've ever seen."

HOW PLAYERS TRY TO BREAK OUT OF A SLUMP

Bill Caudill, Athletics: "When we played for Seattle, Bill took a bunch of the game bats and built a bonfire and burned them," recalls former teammate Ed Vande Berg of the Indians. "After the bat-burning ceremony, we went out and won that night."

Bill Buckner, Red Sox—During the middle of the 1987 season, he shaved off his mustache because he said, "It'll make me young and quick. There were a lot of food particles in there—and a lot of bad luck."

Baltimore Orioles—With his team mired in a 10-game losing streak in 1987, manager Cal Ripkin, Sr., dressed his Orioles in the bright orange uniforms that had last been worn in Baltimore during the team's 1983 world championship season. It worked. In the orange duds, the Orioles snapped their losing skein as well as the Blue Jays' 11-game winning streak with an 8–4 victory. Said Ripkin afterward, "We'll have to take these uniforms home and sleep in them."

Mark Langston, Mariners—In 1986, after suffering through nine straight starts without a win, Langston threw away his glove and got a new hat and new shoes. Then he went out and twirled a five-hitter to beat the Yankees.

Ozzie Guillen, White Sox: "Ozzie wears his pants pretty high," says teammate Steve Lyons. "But one day he wanted to change his luck so he decided to wear his pants down low the way Don Mattingly wears them. Oz got five hits that night."

Montreal Expos: "Some of the guys will use different stalls or urinals to change their luck," says Wallace Johnson of the Expos. "They'll say, 'This urinal doesn't have any [good luck]. I'm going to use this other one.'"

♦

Ron Kittle, Yankees: "Once when he was trying to break out of a bad slump, he put war paint on his face," said former teammate Greg Walker of the White Sox. "He had eye black all over his face—but it didn't help."

Brian Fisher, Pirates—After going nearly a month without a victory in 1987, the hurler got a buzzed haircut like the one Arnold Schwarzenegger wore in the movie *Predator.* The next day, Fisher hurled a shutout. Coach Tommy Sandt said Fisher's personality changed with the haircut. "He was a killer out there. Every inning he'd come into the dugout screaming and shouting. He was wild."

Seattle Mariners: "When I was with the team in 1985," says Jack Lazorko of the Angels, "we went into a bad slump, so [manager] Chuck Cottier picked the lineup right out of the hat. We still lost."

Toronto Blue Jays: "Before we became a pennant contender," says Lloyd Moseby, "a lot of guys used to say, 'Let's turn our luck around' and then they'd turn their jerseys inside out or they'd put their left foot in their right shoe and right foot in their left shoe." Adds Jesse Barfield, "When we had a losing streak, some of the guys decided to wear the same clothes without washing them until we won. Let me tell you, I wanted to win bad because I didn't want to smell them."

Mark Grant, Padres: "When I had a pitching slump, I changed athletic supporters and cups. Another time, I tried growing a mustache. It wasn't a very good one. The first time I went out to the mound with one, I got hit with a one-hopper in the ankle. The next inning, I got hit with a one-hopper in the chin. That did it. After the inning, I went into the clubhouse and shaved off my mustache."

▲

BAD LUCK

Reserve Jim Pankovits of the Astros was batting only .122 early in the 1987 season when he became desperate for a way to break out of his slump. "Jim threw his bat in our clubhouse chapel, hoping for a miracle, I guess," recalls an Astro. "Then [trainer] Doc Ewell said, 'I remember a guy did that back in the 1950s and the next day he was shipped to Omaha.' Two days later, Pankovits was sent to Tacoma."

Rangers manager Bobby Valentine doesn't ignore chain letters anymore. He was sent one just before the 1987 season started, but he tossed it aside and forgot about it. However, the day after the Rangers blew a three-run ninth-inning lead to lose their ninth straight game, Valentine found the letter among some old mail. Not wanting to take any chances, the manager made 20 copies of the letter and sent them to other managers and players to fulfill the requirements of the chain letter. That night, the Rangers beat Baltimore 6–4 to snap their losing streak.

"When I go out on the field to third base," says Keith Moreland of the Cubs, "I usually pick up the ball and toss it to the pitcher. Boy, the first time I did that to Ed Lynch, he let the ball roll all the way to the dugout. He told me not to touch that ball, that only *he* could pick it up because otherwise it was bad luck."

Said Buddy Biancalana of the Royals, "I asked Kevin Seitzer to play catch with me before the game and he wouldn't do it. He said it was bad luck." A week later, Biancalana was shipped back to the minors.

WHAT STRANGE THINGS DO PLAYERS CARRY OR WEAR ON THE FIELD?

Rob Murphy, Reds: "I never leave the bullpen without my black silk underwear firmly in place. My grandmother bought me some new ones [during the 1987 season], but I gave up runs in four straight appearances so it was back to the old ones."

DeWayne Buice, Angels: "I keep a picture of [bullpen coach] Bob Clear under my hat. He's always telling me to keep the ball down, and so when I'm on the mound and struggling a little bit, I take off my hat and look at him. It's a reminder. The picture is frayed and sweated on; it's wet and ugly. I'm trying to get the rest of the pitchers on the team to carry photos of Bob in their hats."

Jerry Royster, White Sox: "I carry a four-leaf clover. In 1973, I was playing AAA ball in Albuquerque where I met this nice family that came to almost every home game. They had three kids under the age of nine. About the second week of the season, one of the kids picked a four-leaf clover in their yard and brought it to me. I put it in my pocket and had one of my best games ever. Since that day, the family has consistently sent me four-leaf clovers. Each one is taped to a piece of paper and that's what I carry. And you know what? The little boy who first gave me the four-leaf clover has just graduated from Texas Tech."

Sammy Stewart, Indians: "I often carry a country buckeye [nut] in my back pocket for good luck. If I find a penny, I'll kiss it and keep it on me when I pitch."

Mike Pagliarulo, Yankees—For over a year, he wore a red ribbon on his jock. "It's an old Italian custom and it was given to me by my grandmother," he said. "It was supposed to keep the evil spirits away."

John Franco, Reds: "Franco carries a stone from his mother's grave when he plays," says Reds beat writer Greg Hoard. "His mother, whom he was very devoted to, died in Brooklyn in 1986. Since then, on New York trips, he visits her grave and picks up a stone to keep as a remembrance."

Greg Swindell, Indians: "Greg carries a big heavy brass belt buckle of a Texas longhorn in his back pocket," says teammate Scott Bailes. "It's from where he went to school."

Joe Niekro, Twins: "I always carry a picture of my son Lance in my back pocket."

Kevin Seitzer, Royals: "He picked up a Coke cup on the field, crushed it, and put it in his back pocket—and his first time at bat afterward, he hit a homer," recalls teammate Bret Saberhagen. "He said he was going to carry the cup with him on the field until things got bad. He got rid of it after his first 0–for game."

Scott Bailes, Indians: "I must wear the same T-shirt on the days I pitch and no matter how hot it is, I have to wear my long thermal underwear."

Rob Deer, Brewers: "He's got to have his wrist bands and plenty of eye black or it seems he can't play," says teammate Dan Plesac. "We joke about it with him. We told him he probably didn't go to his high school prom without his eye black and wrist bands."

Dave Parker, Reds—Parker wears a lucky penny around his neck. The coin belonged to former Tigers scout Chuck Tuzzeo, who had it since 1940 before giving it to Parker in 1985. Tuzzeo said the penny—which was blessed at the Vatican, at Fatima, and at the Shrine of Guadalupe—"carried me through two wars and 109 missions. I've survived seven heart bypass surgeries." He told Parker to "rub this coin when you need its help and it will respond." Right after putting it on, Parker hit in 13 straight games.

▲
EATING ON THE JOB

Although pitchers are notorious for smuggling food into the bullpen during a game, Mark Brouhard of the Brewers managed to sneak a snack while playing in left field.

"Mark took a donut out with him in left," recalls teammate Jim Gantner. "He hid it in his back pocket and every once in a while, he'd pull it out and take a bite out of it." Adds teammate Bill Schroeder, "That's the weirdest thing I've ever seen a player carry with him during a game."

WHAT DIRTY TRICKS DO GROUNDSKEEPERS EMPLOY TO HELP THE HOME TEAM?

1. **Tilting the foul lines**
2. **Tailoring the grass**
3. **Wetting down the base paths**
4. **Doctoring the home plate area**
5. **Tampering with the pitcher's mound**

If you look carefully at the playing field, you might spot the handiwork of the doctors of dirt—the groundskeepers. They do more than just tend to the grass and base paths. Sometimes they tailor the field to accommodate the strengths and weaknesses of the home team while trying to neutralize the strengths of the opposition. According to the *Baseball Confidential* survey, players have grounds for complaints about the following:

Tilting the Foul Lines

Home teams blessed with speedsters and good bunters want foul lines graded slightly inward so that a bunted ball rolling down the line tends to stay fair. "At Arlington Stadium, on the third-base line, they dug a thin groove in between the grass and the foul line so if you bunt anything that starts fair, it ends up fair," says Marty Barrett of the Red Sox. The White Sox's Steve Lyons claims that at Anaheim Stadium, "They run the grass right up to the foul line, figuring that when their guys bunt, the ball has a good chance of hitting the edge of the grass and staying fair."

If a club doesn't possess speed and is unlikely to bunt much, the grade of the foul lines will often be slightly outward, causing the ball to roll foul. "If you bunt a ball even close to the line at Tiger Stadium, it's going to go foul," admits Kirk Gibson of the Tigers.

Tailoring the Grass

Groundskeepers grow the grass tall and thick for teams with slow-footed fielders and low-ball pitchers. "Our grass is long in the outfield and I like it that way," says Gibson, who plays left field. "I feel more confident about charging a ball because I know the ball is less likely to take a quick bounce on me in tall grass. If a ball is hit in the power alley, I have a better chance of cutting it off before it rolls all the way to the wall."

The Tiger infield grass grows tall, as does the turf at Wrigley Field, Candlestick Park, and Fenway Park to slow down grounders. "The Cubs' infield had even taller grass a few years ago when they had Ron Cey at third and Larry Bowa at short," said an Astro. "They were at the end of their careers and they were slow, so the left side of the infield looked like a hay field that hadn't been mowed."

Rich Dotson of the White Sox says tall grass—the kind grown in Comiskey Park—is a friend of sinkerball pitchers who coax batters into hitting grounders. "Tall grass slows ground balls and keeps them in the infield where the guys can make the plays." Adds Tim Flannery of the Padres, "With [Giants manager] Roger Craig, you'll find the grass is always thick and tall because his teams have pitchers who throw the split-fingered fastball and get batters to hit lots of ground balls."

Teams with quick, fast infielders prefer seeing the grass given a razor cut so that it's as fast as a freshly mowed green. "In Texas," says Jack Lazorko of the Angels, "the grass is so short it's almost like AstroTurf."

Wetting Down the Base Paths

To neutralize the speed of opposing teams, groundskeepers water down the base paths, especially the takeoff area next to first base. The Braves, for instance, are generally slow-footed, so they make sure the dirt part of the infield is turned into a swamp, according to several players. "The Cubs and Giants do the same thing," claims Tim Raines of the Expos. "Since they don't run very well, they want to make it hard for other teams that like to run." Jesse Barfield of the Blue Jays complains that the base paths in Detroit and Boston are too slow. "We have guys who can run fast, and when we go there, the track is slow and that's to the advantage of those teams because they don't have many base-stealing threats."

By the same token, fast teams such as the Cardinals keep hard, fast tracks. "The base paths in St. Louis are like cement," says an Expo. "If ever a team is in the fast lane, it's the Cardinals."

Doctoring the Home Plate Area

Groundskeepers tailor the ground around the home plate area to fit the skills of the home team's pitchers and hitters. For example, says Tim Raines, "Montreal leaves the area in front of home plate hard, which means hitters get better bounces when they chop down on the ball. The Expos are fast and can beat out a lot of hits from high choppers." It's no different at Busch Stadium, says Tim Flannery. "It's as hard as a rock and all those speedy Cardinals have to do is chop down on the ball and they've got a hit."

To combat those high-bounding choppers, groundskeepers mix the dirt around the home plate area with layers of sand. "We do that in Detroit," says Kirk Gibson. "We're not a chop, chop, and run team. We're a club that drives the ball and hits home runs rather than beats the ball into the ground." The sand also thwarts grounders from scooting through the infield, says Tom Brunansky of the Twins. "In most parks, there's usually hard dirt between home plate and the start of the grass. But in Detroit, they soften it up with sand to slow things up and that helps their infield."

Sinkerball pitchers want the front of home plate watered down, says Jack Lazorko. "Whenever Tommy John [of the Yankees] pitches in New York, you can bet the front of the plate is all watered down." Such a soaking can also help fast teams, says Gibson. "In Cleveland, the bunting area in front of the plate is so soaked it's unbelievable. They do it because guys like Brett Butler and Otis Nixon are dropping bunts down all the time. If the pitcher fields the ball, he can't throw it because he's going to fall on his ass."

Tampering with the Pitcher's Mound

Some groundskeepers love to mess with opposing hurlers' minds by altering the pitcher's mound. For example, a few inches might be shaved off or added onto the mound in the visitor's bullpen. "They sometimes make the bullpen mound steeper or not as steep as the mound on the field," says Ed Vande Berg of the Indians. "That can sure screw up a pitcher coming into the game. It might take him a few pitches to adjust to the regular mound." Since each pitch is crucial to a reliever in a tight situation, this trick can be especially devious. Scott McGregor of the Orioles claims that sometimes when he is slated to pitch on the road, he will notice that the mound has been tampered with. "I pitch off to the side a little, and it's easy for them to slant the mound in a way to make it uncomfortable for me."

Groundskeepers can also mold the mound to benefit the home team's pitching staff. "If a team has hard throwers, the mound will be raised a little bit to give them a little more leverage and more speed on the ball," says Mike Boddicker of the Orioles.

BEST INFIELD TO PLAY ON

1. Dodger Stadium, Los Angeles
2. Fenway Park, Boston
3. Jack Murphy Stadium, San Diego
4. Exhibition Stadium, Toronto
5. Busch Stadium, St. Louis

WORST INFIELD TO PLAY ON

1. Astrodome, Houston
2. Municipal Stadium, Cleveland
3. The Coliseum, Oakland
4. Yankee Stadium, New York
5. Wrigley Field, Chicago

WHOM DO PLAYERS AVOID DURING A BENCH-CLEARING BRAWL?

Gary Gaetti, Twins: "Don Baylor. He's very powerful. I was in the middle of a pile-up in 1982 when I was a rookie. Baylor wanted to get in the middle of it and I was in his way so he flicked me aside and I was thrown five feet away. That made a real impression on me."

DeWayne Buice, Angels: "George Bell. I heard he's got a black belt in karate and that's good enough reason for me to stay clear of him."

Tony Gwynn, Padres: "Lee Smith and Dave Winfield. For me, trying to go up against those guys, I have no chance. Even if I carry a bat with me, I have no chance."

Mike Easler, Yankees: "Players who've been in the league a long time, like George Brett, Dave Winfield, and Mike Schmidt. They have a lot of class. Get the young guys."

Charlie Kerfeld, Astros: "Dave Parker. If the two of us started fighting, it would be like two pro wrestlers hitting the ground. The earth would be shaking."

Gary Lucas, Angels: "Bo Jackson. Not only is he capable of slamming me to the ground, but if I happen to run away from him, I think he could outrun me."

Tom Candiotti, Indians: "Jose Canseco. He'd tear your head off."

Bill Madlock, Tigers: "Rob Deer. I saw him pick up Joe Niekro and body-slam him. Also, Kirk Gibson. You can see it in his eyes when he gets mad. He turns into a psycho."

Kent Tekulve, Phillies: "Big guys like Dave Parker and Mike Schmidt because they normally don't get into brawls, but when they do, you know they're really upset and they're serious. A lot of times, guys aren't serious. They just join in the pile to showboat."

Scott Bailes, Indians: "George Bell, because one time I saw a pitcher with George Bell's spike marks in his chest."

Tom Paciorek, Rangers: "I wouldn't want to get in a brawl with a real little guy, especially if he beat me up. That would be embarrassing."

NICE GUY

How well liked is Braves' superstar Dale Murphy around the league?

"Let me give you an example," says Terry Francona of the Reds. "During a bench-clearing brawl between the Reds and the Braves [in

1987], Dale got an elbow right in the chops. After everything had settled down, about four or five Reds went up to him and asked if he was all right."

▲
OFF-BASE CONVERSATIONS

Players in the *Baseball Confidential* survey were asked to give examples of strange things opposing players have told them during a game. Here are some of their answers:

Gary Gaetti, Twins: "When I was called up from the minors in 1981, George Brett came over and tried to rattle me in a good-humored way. He pointed to the crowd and told me, 'You know what? I hate every one of those fuckers in the stands—except for those three girls over there.' "

Gary Lucas, Angels: "I've been throwing a split-fingered fast-ball that I developed in 1986, but my friend Terry Kennedy [of the Orioles] hadn't seen it because he hadn't faced me since 1985. Well, the first time I threw it to him in 1987, he grounded out. As he was running back to the dugout, he said to me, 'Why the fuck didn't you tell me you were throwing that pitch?' "

Kent Tekulve, Phillies: "Before a game in Philadelphia, Terry Francona [of the Reds] asked if his dad Tito [a former major leaguer] could play in a celebrity golf tournament that I was organizing. I said sure and arranged to have an invitation sent to Tito. The following week, we were playing in Cincy and I faced Terry. He hit a little dribbler up the first-base line. I fielded the ball and tagged him out. Then I said, 'Your dad's letter is in the mail.' He did a double take as I headed back to the mound. The next day, before the game, Terry came up to me and asked, 'What did you say to me yesterday?' I told him, 'Your dad's letter is in the mail.' Terry then said, 'I thought you said it was a horseshit hit.' And I replied, 'It was a horseshit hit, but that wasn't what I told you.' "

Mike Boddicker, Orioles: "Jim Rice had just flied out, and as he crossed the mound to go back to the dugout, he told me, 'Gee, I haven't hit off you for the last two games. Why don't you throw me a fastball inside sometime so I can get a base hit!' "

Pat Clements, Yankees: "In my rookie year, I got Bill Buckner out three straight times. After the third time, he screamed at me, 'You'll never get me out again!' I didn't say anything and the next time up, he hit a weak pop-up four feet in front of the plate. I still didn't say anything."

Bryn Smith, Expos: "Manny Trillo [of the Cubs] and I communicate with each other from our dugouts. We use gestures. He tells me how far he's going to hit it off me and I tell him he's going to get hit before he hits anything off me."

▲

LEFT SPEECHLESS

Floyd Rayford of the Orioles, who has hit Red Sox hurler Oil Can Boyd like he owns him, recalls a conversation he had with him in 1986:

"I was 9 for 17 off Oil Can when we bumped into each other at a disco. He asked me, 'How come you always hit me?' I said, 'I don't know, man. I'm just lucky I guess.' And then he asked, 'What do I have to do to get you out?' I said, 'Throw the ball down the middle with nothing on it—about 83 miles an hour.' Two days later I faced him. His first pitch to me was right down the middle with nothing on it. I took it. His second pitch was the same as the first and I hit it up into the bleachers. We haven't talked since."

OFF
THE
FIELD

WHO ARE THE BIGGEST CHOWHOUNDS IN BASEBALL?

Dwight Gooden, Mets: "He made aviation history in 1985 when he ate six airplane meals on one flight," says teammate Doug Sisk. "He just unsnapped his pants, laid back, and groaned." Adds former teammate Ed Lynch of the Cubs: "I've seen Dwight put away two super-sized porterhouse steaks, two baked potatoes, and two salads at one sitting. Most of us couldn't even finish one of those steaks. The waiters stood around in awe."

Jerry Reed, Mariners: "I was voted the International League's 'Spread Killer of the Year' two years in a row. Here's a list of my five favorite restaurants on the road: No. 1, McDonald's off Main Street in Milwaukee; No. 2, McDonald's off State Street in Minneapolis; No. 3, McDonald's across the street from the Double Tree in Anaheim; No. 4, McDonald's in Times Square in New York City; and No. 5, Burger King in Kansas City near our hotel—because there's no McDonald's close by."

Mark Eichhorn, Blue Jays: "After an afternoon game on the road, he'll eat the spread, then get a meal or two on the plane, and then figure out where he's going to eat a third dinner," says teammate Kelly Gruber.

Frank Viola and Mark Davidson, Twins: "The cafeteria has no chance with those two," says teammate George Frazier.

Tommy Lasorda, Dodgers manager: "When he eats in his office after the game, it's like King Henry the Eighth," says Cincinnati beat writer Greg Hoard. "He can polish off tons and tons of ribs with sauce dripping everywhere and running down his sleeves. He's more interested in eating after the game than in conducting any postgame press conference. It's disgusting."

Chris James, Phillies: "It's not that he sits down and eats a lot at one sitting," says teammate Don Carman. "He just never stops eating."

Jim Sundberg, Cubs: "Sundberg will eat the spread and then go out for dinner that night and have a full-course meal," says former teammate Dan Quisenberry of the Royals. Adds Buddy Biancalana, "Jim and I were at a crab place in Baltimore where Jim ordered a dozen crabs, some crab cakes, and some softshell crab sandwiches. It was so much that the waitress couldn't fit all his food on the table. She had to put it on a serving cart."

Roger McDowell, Mets: "My typical order at McDonald's is two Quarter Pounders with cheese, a Big Mac, a fish sandwich, two cheeseburgers, a large order of french fries, a large iced tea, a vanilla milkshake, and a piece of cherry pie." Why only one order of fries? "I need room for the cherry pie."

Charlie Kerfeld, Astros: "Charlie eats and drinks anything," says former teammate Bill Dawley of the Cardinals. "He never met a plate of food he didn't like. He always says he's going on a diet. His diet consists of four hotdogs and a mountain of food."

Shane Mack, Padres: "He's Mr. Chowhound by far," says teammate Tony Gwynn. "One day, he brought a bag with two sandwiches and ate it at the park. Then he fixed two hotdogs in the clubhouse and ate those. After BP, he had two ice cream bars. Then after the game, he had two helpings of fish and six or seven Cokes."

Eric King, Tigers: "We call him 'Super Slug,' " says teammate Kirk Gibson. "He's got to have a sandwich every other inning. When we have a doubleheader, I'll go up to him and say, 'This is going to be a pretty tough day for you—you've got to eat for two games.' "

Rick Reuschel, Giants: "They call him 'Big Daddy' for a reason," says Ryne Sandberg of the Cubs. "During the 1987 All-Star Game, Rick pitched one of the middle innings and then went into the clubhouse. When Lee Smith came into the game and it went into extra innings, we were joking that Lee—who's a big chowhound himself—was out on the mound trying to get the game over with because he knew that Rick was in the clubhouse digging into the spread."

Ron Hassey, Yankees: "He's always eating wherever he goes," says a teammate. "Sometimes he'll sneak into the clubhouse and grab a couple of ribs during a game. But that's not bad because when he does that, he usually gets a hit. 'Ribs for hits,' I always say."

WHAT KIND OF SHENANIGANS DO PLAYERS PULL ON PLANES?

Maybe it's the altitude; maybe it's the boredom. But as players fly tens of thousands of miles a season, they often need to cut loose. After all, they can read only so many magazines and sleep only so many hours.

"Things can get crazy in the air," says Steve Lyons of the White Sox, "especially on charter flights when we have the plane to ourselves. Grown men start acting like 10-year-olds. Take 'aisle skiing,' for instance. You know those plastic-coated cards in the pouches of the seat backs that tell you where the exits are? Well, on charter flights, you put two of them in the aisle and stand on them. Then when the plane takes off, you 'ski' down the aisle toward the back of the plane."

Here are some other ways players pass the time on team flights:

Tom Brunansky, Twins: "We attach fishing line to a 10- or 20-dollar bill and place it on the floor. When people stoop down to pick it up, we jerk it away from them. It's always good for a laugh."

Tim Flannery, Padres: "Teammates have handcuffed me to my seat after I've fallen asleep on the plane. Once I woke up and had the headphones on and someone had taken the plug and stuck it in my mouth. I had my mouth open and I was snoring as loud as could be. Passengers were taking pictures of me and everything. I felt like an idiot when I woke up."

Roger McDowell, Mets: "You go to the lavatory and get a sanitary napkin and then mark it up with a red felt-tip pen. Then you walk down the aisle and slap it on the back of some unsuspecting guy and you walk on. He doesn't realize he has a bloody-looking Kotex stuck to his back. We've done that on commercial flights. Another one is to buy a vial of that sulfur-smelling stuff and tape it to the bottom of the toilet seat of the airplane. Then you gently lower the seat down. The next person who sits on it breaks the vial and stinks up the whole lavatory worse than ever."

Jim Gantner, Brewers: "When you fall asleep, they take your shoes and you have to walk off the plane with no shoes on. I know. It's happened to me."

Steve Lyons, White Sox: "When I was with the Red Sox and they served grapes on the flight, the guys in the back would start a grape fight. Grapes would fly all over. I tried to stay out of these fights because I figured the grapes would stain my clothes and I didn't make the kind of money that those guys were making. They can afford to buy all the shirts they want."

Angels player: "Sometimes a player will wear one of those ugly masks on the plane. Bobby Grich had one with an eyeball hanging out and he would scare passengers. One time, the team boarded the plane first and Bobby put on the mask and hid behind his aisle seat. Then the regular passengers came on board and the first one was a little old lady. Bobby jumped out at her and she just about lost it. We loved it. It's funny—in a demented sort of way."

Bob Gibson, Mets: "On some planes, when guys go to the bathroom, you can pull the seat back far enough so that it blocks the door and they aren't able to get out."

Peter Schmuck, Los Angeles beat writer: "For the macabre, nothing tops what [former catcher] Tom Donohue did. He was going to be a mortician and he'd bring his books with him to study. On this real turbulent flight, when some of the players were getting a little worried, Tom began reading out loud from a book about how to prepare the charred remains of crash victims. By now, the plane was really getting tossed around. So Tom reached in his briefcase and pulled out a handful of coroner's toe tags—the kind they put on corpses in the morgue—and began handing them out to the players. He told them, 'At least we could be courteous.' It just freaked everybody out."

LET SLEEPING ROOKIES LIE

Who says players treat rookies badly? Look how thoughtful the Padres were when Lance McCullers was first called up to the team in 1985.

McCullers fell asleep during the team's bus ride from Kennedy Airport to Manhattan. Upon reaching the hotel, the players decided not to disrupt his slumber. They quietly tiptoed off the bus with their gear. The bus then headed back to its terminal.

"I woke up about two miles from the bus station, and the bus driver was sure startled to see me," said McCullers, who now knows better than to ever sleep on the team bus. The driver obligingly delivered McCullers back to the hotel around three A.M., more than an hour after the rest of the players were bedded down.

THE FOUR BEST PRANKS PULLED ON PLAYERS IN THEIR HOTEL ROOMS

Players are always pulling practical jokes on each other in their hotels. Among the usual pranks are leaving 5 A.M. wake-up calls for teammates after a long night game, placing weird and disgusting things in each other's beds, and throwing water and baby powder on players when they open their hotel-room door.

But according to the *Baseball Confidential* survey, the hotel pranks considered the best are the following:

Victim: Wilfredo Tejada, Expos rookie: "The team was in a Cincinnati hotel where Tejada was rooming with Luis Rivera," recalls Montreal beat writer Wesley Goldstein. "About two A.M., one of the players pounded on the door and yelled for Tejada to come to the door. When Tejada opened the door, his roomie, Rivera, pushed him out into the hallway and locked the door. The other players had all fled back to their rooms and locked their doors. Tejada was left standing in his underwear in the hallway. Then one of the players called hotel security and said, 'There's a crazed homosexual running around the eighth floor in his underwear. You better take care of it.' Hotel security grabbed Tejada and brought him down to the manager's office. But since Tejada had trouble speaking English, it took quite a while before everything was straightened out. It was sort of his welcome to the majors."

Victim: Rene Lachemann, Mariners manager: "It happened in Chicago," says prime suspect Bill Caudill, now with the Athletics. "A couple of guys broke into Lachemann's hotel room when he was out to dinner. They took all his furniture and flipped it over. They took the mouthpiece out of his telephone, stole every light bulb and towel in the room, and put Vaseline on the inside doorknob so that once he got in, he couldn't get out. Then they put Jell-0 in the toilet and poured ice from the ice machine in the toilet so it would harden quickly. When Lachemann returned to his room and the lights didn't work, he thought there had been a power failure so he went into the bathroom. He peed on Jell-0. Then he noticed that his bed and everything had been flipped over. When he tried to call the front desk, he could hear them but they couldn't hear him." Despite overwhelming evidence to the contrary, Caudill insists, "I had nothing to do with it." This from a man who has a history of ransacking rooms. Says former teammate Ed Vande Berg of the Indians, "One night while [Mariners broadcaster] Dave Niehaus was gone, Bill and I ransacked his room and put everything in his bathroom and removed the phone. When Niehaus returned, we shoved a penny in the lock of his door and he couldn't get out."

Victim: Steve Sax, Dodgers: After a few Dodgers had attended a party in Philadelphia where their host had roasted a pig, they got this great idea. They confiscated the pig's head, put it in a sack, and smuggled it into the team's hotel. Somehow they sneaked into Sax's room when he wasn't there and placed the head of the pig on one of Sax's pillows. They also left a note. The culprits pulled up the bedspread, turned out the lights and crept back to their rooms. When Sax returned, he turned on a light in the bathroom but not the one near his bed. A few minutes later, he slid beneath the sheets and suddenly felt something fleshy. He turned on the light and stared right into the face of a pig. Once Sax's heart started beating again, he picked up the note. It read: "You'd better start playing better. The Godfather."

Victim: Reggie Cleveland, Brewers: When Cleveland returned to his Kansas City hotel room, he saw a card on the bed. It said, "Please autograph my pig." Cleveland couldn't figure out what the message meant until moments later when a squealing piglet scampered out from under his bed. "Bob McClure [now with the Expos] was behind it," says Jim Gantner of the Brewers. "Reggie shipped the pig home to his ranch in Texas and had his wife send him pictures of the pig as it grew up."

▲

HAVING A BALL

Some players take their bats to their hotel rooms and practice swinging in front of a mirror. Phillies relief pitcher Kent Tekulve takes a baseball.

"I've been known to take a ball to bed with me," he says. "Every once in a while I'll go through a phase where the ball doesn't feel good in my hand. So I'll take a ball and keep it in my hand all night to get that feel back. Believe it or not, it works for me."

▲

PLAYERS WHO MAKE FASHION MIS-STATEMENTS

Charlie Kerfeld, Astros: "He doesn't care how he looks coming to the ball park," says former teammate Bill Dawley of the Cardinals. "He wears pink high-tops, holes in his jeans, or a Rambo fatigue outfit." Adds an Astros teammate, "In Atlanta once, Charlie threw up on his shoes and didn't clean them off. Nolan Ryan told him, 'If you don't clean up your act, you're not lockering next to me anymore.' "

Ron Davis, Cubs: "He doesn't know how to tie a tie," says former teammate Kirby Puckett of the Twins. "When he was with us, he had someone else make a knot in his tie for him and then he wouldn't undo it for the whole year. He'd just slip it over his head."

Kent Tekulve, Phillies: "He's very bold," says a teammate. "He's not afraid to mix plaids with stripes."

Doug Sisk, Mets: "With Doug, nothing matches and nothing is ironed," says teammate Roger McDowell. "He looks like he irons his clothes with a Belgian waffle iron. Dougie did buy this one real nice silk suit—you know, the kind that looks like you spilled lacquer on it. The first time he wore it on the plane, he sat down and the seat ripped out."

Dave Parker, Reds: "Parker dresses really well, but he has on so many rings and chains that he looks like a display window at a jewelry store," says a teammate.

Pete Rose, Reds manager: "Pete wears pants that look like they were painted on him," says a beat writer. "It's incredible. I mean, he has them tailored but the tailor must be working from 1968 specs."

Ruppert Jones, Angels: "He's always had a flair for wearing the unusual," says teammate Gary Lucas. "Some of the players have told him that they come to the clubhouse early just to see what he's wearing each day. He's got an outfit that has red and white stripes going down the jacket and blue satin pants. It makes him look like he works at the popcorn machine at Disneyland."

Rick Cerone, Yankees: "Some of the Yankees say that for all the money Rick makes, he's got to be the worst-dressed player in baseball," says teammate Wayne Tolleson. "He wears these loud sports coats with different-colored Converse All-Stars."

Sportswriters: "They can't put two colors together, I know that," claims Gary Gaetti of the Twins.

SOAPS GET IN THEIR EYES

Some of the most loyal fans of daytime soap operas are baseball players. It's understandable. Since most games are played at night and players sleep late, they have hours to kill before going to the park. So they watch TV soaps.

"When I'm on the road, I get up at 11 A.M. and watch five or six soap operas in a row," says the Twins' All-Star outfielder Kirby Puckett. "*All My Children* is my favorite."

During the 1987 season, several Cardinals showed up at the New York sets of two ABC daytime dramas, *One Life to Live* and *All My Children*. The players watched the shooting of several scenes, including a love scene that left one Card muttering, "If only I could do that and get paid for it."

THE FRIENDLIEST GUYS IN BASEBALL

1. Dale Murphy
2. Kirby Puckett
3. George Brett
4. Paul Molitor
5. Mookie Wilson

WHICH PLAYERS ARE TOTALLY UNLIKE THEIR PUBLIC IMAGE?

George Brett, Royals: "I don't know how I ever got this image as an All-American boy next door. I'm the opposite. I like to dress like a slob and be a slob."

Bert Blyleven, Twins: "Here's a man who does a lot of crazy things, says a lot of crazy things, and has flipped off the crowd," says Rick Sutcliffe of the Cubs. "Yet he's probably one of the kindest, most giving persons I've ever run across. He's got a big heart. Any charity, any person who needs help, Bert is the first to offer it."

George Bell, Blue Jays: "On the field and in the press, George gives the impression that he's real mean and unfriendly, but that's not a true picture of him," says teammate Tom Henke. "He's a very easygoing, nice guy who makes everybody laugh and keeps the clubhouse loose."

Joaquin Andujar, Athletics: "He's portrayed as a big hothead on the mound and it's true he does lose his temper now and then," says a former teammate. "Okay, he's a hotdog too. But there's another side to him. He has a heart of gold. Every year he goes back to the Dominican Republic [where he was born] and brings shipments of shoes and clothes for poor children and equipment to kids who want to play baseball. He also buys lots of food for the hungry. And when he won 20 games in 1985, he gave thousand-dollar checks to the players who helped him win his 20th."

Eddie Murray, Orioles: "He has this image that he doesn't like anybody, won't talk to anybody, and doesn't care about anything," says teammate Mike Boddicker. "He's the opposite of that. He is kind and he does things for people that no one else knows about. He's fabulous with kids. He does his good deeds in a quiet way."

Goose Gossage, Padres: "Goose has an image of being a tough, aggressive guy and not real friendly because of the way he acts on the mound," says former teammate Terry Kennedy of the Orioles. "But off the field, he's one of the greatest guys you'd ever want to meet. He's a family man who loves to spend time with his kids and hunt and fish with them."

Willie Upshaw, Blue Jays: "On the field, Willie plays hard-nosed baseball, screams at the umpire, has an aggressive style about him," says teammate Lloyd Moseby. "But off the field, he's an introvert and pretty shy. When we go out in public and people try to talk to him, he doesn't say anything. They think he's snobbish or something. He's not. He's just an introvert."

Tom Seaver: "He has this clean-cut, All-American, conservative image, but he'll do anything when he's with the guys," says former teammate Ray Knight of the Orioles. "One time, I invited him down to Georgia for some hunting. There were several state legislators with us and we were driving in two jeeps. Tom was in the jeep ahead of us and he dropped his pants and mooned us."

▲

BIG HIT

Like many altruistic players, Glenn Hubbard of the Braves spends some of his free time cheering up seriously ill children. But few big leaguers have ever been able to honor the kids' most common request: "Hit a homer for me."

During the 1987 season, a group called Magic Moments arranged for blind, seven-year-old Steve Clark, who had undergone two kidney transplants, to attend a Braves game and meet Hubbard, his favorite player. Hubbard gave the boy a ball, bat, and a generous amount of his time. As Hubbard was leaving, Steve asked, "Will you hit a homer for me?" Even though Hubbard is a singles hitter, he replied, "I'll try. You never know what will happen."

To the everlasting joy of little Steve, Hubbard blasted his third homer of the season as the Braves won 2–1. "Funny how things work out," Hubbard said. "We as players should be able to do something to make a difference in their [kids'] lives. I'm happy for him."

THE
FRONT
OFFICE

WHAT TEAM RULES DO PLAYERS FIND THE MOST RIDICULOUS?

1. **Restrictive dress codes**
2. **Bans on alcohol in the clubhouse and on flights**
3. **Curfews**
4. **Limitations on facial hair**

Most owners and managers believe that discipline off the field is one of the keys to winning. As a result, each club has instituted its own rules. Although the players, for the most part, follow the rules, they find some of them ridiculous—especially restrictive dress codes.

All teams require their players to wear sport coats on travel days. Surprisingly, while National League clubs don't insist on ties, all American League clubs do—with the exception of the Blue Jays, Rangers, Royals, Tigers, and Red Sox. "The stupidest rule ever is having to wear ties on flights," declares Tom Candiotti of the Indians. "Baseball players don't know how to dress anyway, and you get all kinds of funny ties and none of them match the sport coats."

But, according to the *Baseball Confidential* survey, ties aren't the biggest dress issue with players—socks are. "Having to wear socks on the plane is the dumbest rule I've ever heard," says Tony Gwynn of the Padres. "If you wear a suit and tie, nobody is going to look at your feet." White Sox management requires its players to arrive at the ball park with socks on their feet. "The player ought to feel comfortable going to the park, but the boss makes us wear socks," says Chicago's Ozzie Guillen. "Most players feel uncomfortable with socks." Several White Sox players and Twins have been fined for not wearing socks to the ball park.

Another bone of contention over dress codes is the ban on jeans on flights. "I don't think it's right that we can't wear nice jeans on flights," says Rick Manning of the Brewers, which has such a rule. Adds another player, "I've got jeans that are more expensive, nicer looking, and more comfortable than some of my slacks, but I can't wear them when we travel and that's absurd. I wish the front office would wake up and realize what century we're in."

Although drinking policies vary greatly from team to team, an increasing number of clubs have banned alcohol in the clubhouse and on flights. Alcohol is not allowed in the Angels, White Sox, and Padres clubhouses, and on the White Sox, Tigers, Dodgers, Angels and Pirates team flights.

"The silliest team rule is no drinking in the clubhouse," says Jerry Royster of the White Sox. "You're dealing with guys who are over 21. When I played at San Diego, the club told Graig Nettles, who was 40 at the time, that he couldn't have a beer after the game. Can you believe it?" Adds Tony Gwynn of the Padres, "Beer has been in the clubhouse since the game was invented, and without it, you feel like you're not part of major league baseball. The no-beer rule is so dumb." After White Sox general manager Larry Himes announced a ban on alcohol in the clubhouse in 1987, catcher Carlton Fisk told the press, "It seemed strange to see guys [in the clubhouse] eating pizza and drinking Sprite. It just doesn't make sense." When Fisk said he would place a cooler of beer inside his locker, which he considers private, Himes actually alerted Comiskey Park security to check Fisk at the gate.

Players with clubs that ban alcohol on team flights sometimes flout the rule. "To be honest with you," admits Kirk Gibson of the Tigers, "I've had liquor on the plane. I've carried my own little bottle with me. I might order ice water from the stewardess and sneak my little bottle of J&B out of my briefcase and have a little nip. I know there are other guys who have taken beer on the plane. [Manager] Sparky Anderson knows that, but he isn't going to say anything about it because we don't get loud or out of hand. The rule is still in effect. Sparky has taught us how to act in public and he gets plenty of compliments on how we behave and look."

If players had their way, there would be no curfews. Several teams have curfews of two to three hours after night games. "Curfews are pretty dumb," says Rick Manning. "Players are grown men and to have somebody tell them what time to be in bed is ridiculous." Adds Frank DiPino of the Cubs, "I'm old enough to take care of myself. I mean, it's not like the guys don't know how to handle themselves at night. It's different if a guy has a problem. The club ought to just give him a curfew."

Hair codes are another irritant to players. "The Tigers had a rule against mustaches when I came up," said Kirk Gibson. "But I decided to grow one because I figured I was old enough to have hair on my face. Sparky has slacked off on that rule."

While the Yankees can have facial hair, players in the club's minor league system can't. "That makes it rough on a veteran who is sent down," says New York beat writer Tom Pedulla. "[Yankees pitcher] Cecilio Guante worked on a goatee for a number of years and prided himself on it. Then he was sent down to the minors. The Yankee rule states you have to arrive at the minor league team clean shaven. So he shaved it off. A couple of weeks later, the Yankees called him back up and when he arrived everyone kidded him about his missing goatee."

Players around the National League have condemned the Reds' front office for its ban on facial hair and long hair. "They're more concerned about the appearance of the player than his performance," says Bill Dawley of the Cardinals.

Players also sympathized with the Braves, who had to put up with the restrictive rules of Eddie Haas when he was their manager. In spring training 1985, he laid down these rules: getting a severe sunburn, $250 fine; missing a 12:30 A.M. curfew, $250; playing cards in the clubhouse, $100. "We also couldn't have loud music," says a member of the Braves. "Basically, it was like a boarding school. Now with [manager] Chuck Tanner here, it's more lax, more like a fraternity."

TEAM RULES

All 26 major league teams were surveyed on their policies concerning beer in the clubhouse, alcohol on team flights, dress codes on flights, facial hair, and curfews. Here are the results:

AMERICAN LEAGUE

ANGELS:
No beer allowed in clubhouse
No alcoholic beverages allowed on flights
Sport coats, ties, and dress slacks required on flights; no jeans
Mustaches allowed; no beards
No curfew

ATHLETICS:
Beer allowed in clubhouse
Any kind of alcoholic beverage allowed on flights
Sport coats and ties required on flights
Facial hair allowed
No curfew

BLUE JAYS:
Beer allowed in clubhouse
Any kind of alcoholic beverages allowed on flights
Sport coats required on flights; ties optional
Facial hair allowed
No curfew

BREWERS:
No beer allowed in clubhouse
Beer and wine allowed on flights
Sport coats and ties required on flights and in hotel lobbies; no jeans
Facial hair allowed
No curfew

INDIANS:
Beer allowed in clubhouse
Beer only allowed on flights
Hotel bars off limits
Sport coats and ties required on flights; sport coats required in hotel lobbies
No beards or long sideburns
Curfew one hour after night game

MARINERS:
Beer allowed in clubhouse
Beer only allowed on flights
Sport coats and ties required on commercial flights
Facial hair allowed
No curfew

ORIOLES:
Beer allowed in clubhouse
Beer only allowed on flights
Sport coats, ties, and dress slacks required on flights
Mustaches allowed; no beards
Curfew two hours after night game

RANGERS:
Beer allowed in clubhouse
Beer only on flights
Sport coats required on flights; ties optional
Facial hair allowed
No curfew

RED SOX:
Beer allowed in clubhouse
Beer only allowed on flights
Sport coats required on flights; ties optional
Facial hair allowed
No curfew

ROYALS:
Beer allowed in clubhouse
Beer and wine only allowed on flights
Coats required on flights; jeans allowed
Neat mustaches and beards allowed
No curfew

TIGERS:
Beer allowed in clubhouse
No alcoholic beverages on flights

Sport coats and shirts with collars required on flights and in hotel lobbies; ties optional
Neat mustaches and beards allowed
No curfew

TWINS:
Beer allowed in clubhouse
Beer and wine only allowed on flights
Sport coats, ties, dress pants, and socks required on flights
Facial hair allowed
No curfew

WHITE SOX:
No beer allowed in clubhouse
No alcoholic beverages allowed on flights
Sport coats, ties, socks required on flights; no jeans
Facial hair must be neat
No curfew

YANKEES:
Beer allowed in clubhouse
Beer only allowed on flights
Sport coats and ties required on flights
Mustaches allowed; no beards
Curfew two hours after night game

NATIONAL LEAGUE

ASTROS:
Beer allowed in clubhouse
Beer only allowed on flights
Sport coats required on flights; dress jeans allowed
Facial hair allowed
No curfew

BRAVES:
Beer allowed in clubhouse

Any alcoholic beverages allowed on flights
Sport coats required on flights
Facial hair allowed
Curfew two hours after night games

CARDINALS:
Beer allowed in clubhouse
Any alcoholic beverage allowed on flights
Collared shirts required on flights
Facial hair allowed
No curfew

CUBS:
Beer allowed in clubhouse
Beer only allowed on flights
Sport coats required on flights; no jeans or sneakers
Facial hair allowed
Curfew two hours after bus returns to hotel after night games

DODGERS:
Beer allowed in clubhouse
No alcoholic beverages on flights
Sport coats required on flights; no jeans
No beards
Curfew if team is playing badly

EXPOS:
Beer allowed in clubhouse
Beer and wine only allowed on flights
Sport coats required on flights; dress jeans allowed
Facial hair allowed
No curfew

GIANTS:
Beer allowed in clubhouse
No alcoholic beverages on flights
Sport coats required on flights

No beards
Curfew two hours after night games

METS:
Beer allowed in clubhouse
Beer only allowed on flights
Sport coats required on flights; dress jeans allowed
Facial hair allowed
Curfew two hours after bus returns to hotel after night games

PADRES:
No beer allowed in clubhouse
Beer only allowed on flights
Sport coats required on flights; no jeans
No beards or Fu Manchu mustaches
Curfew two and a half hours after night games

PHILLIES:
Beer allowed in clubhouse
Beer only allowed on flights
Sport coats required on flights; jeans allowed; no sneakers
Facial hair allowed
Curfew depends on how team is playing

PIRATES:
Beer allowed in clubhouse
No beer allowed on flights
Sport coats required on flights; dress jeans allowed
Facial hair allowed
No curfew

REDS:
Beer allowed in clubhouse
Beer only allowed on flights
Sport coats required on flights
No facial hair
Curfew two hours after bus returns to hotel after night games

SOCKING IT TO 'EM

In his dress-for-success team program, White Sox general manager Larry Himes conducted sock patrols of his players in 1987.

First, he issued low-stirrup blue socks for uniforms, which, almost to a man, the players hated. Then Himes personally checked to make sure players had three inches of blue socks showing below their white pant legs. He fined pitcher Neil Allen $200 for wearing the wrong stirrup socks in two consecutive games, including a start on national TV. "To be honest, I didn't really think about it each time," Allen told the press. "I just grabbed 'em and put 'em on. I can't worry about it. I'm having a terrible year. Socks are the last thing on my mind." In protest, the players pulled up their uniform pants to just below their knees.

Himes's sock patrol also extended to checking players' ankles to make sure they were wearing dress socks to and from the ball park. After a win, Himes actually went into the clubhouse and pulled up Scott Nielsen's pant legs, saw Nielsen wasn't wearing socks, and fined him. Himes also fined Ivan Calderon and Jose DeLeon for the same heinous infraction. The fines totaled $400. Complained one player, "This is minor league stuff."

GOOD OL' WHAT'S HIS NAME

In 1986, during his third major league season, Reds reliever Ron Robinson had known only one owner, Cincinnati's Marge Schott. Unfortunately, she didn't know him.

"It was really bizarre," the hurler recalls. "I was in Kroger's grocery shopping when I ran into Marge. So I said, 'Hi, how are you?' And she said, 'Hi, uh, um, what's your name again?' Geez, I'd only been on her team for three years and she still didn't know who I was." This from a pitcher who appeared in 70 games and had a 10–3 record with 14 saves that year.

CONTRACT DEMANDS

When negotiating a contract with the front office, a player seldom gets what he wants—especially when his demands come from left field.

"We've had some crazy contract demands that we just wouldn't accept," says Lou Gorman, Red Sox general manager. "For instance, a player wanted us to provide him with an apartment in the city and a limousine driver. We've had requests from players that their fathers be scouts. One player wanted us to provide him with a rental car in every city on every road trip."

In 1987, the contract demands that caused the biggest stir among major leaguers came from a 16-year-old Puerto Rican pitcher and Bo Jackson of the Royals.

When the Brewers began negotiating with hot prospect Ramser Correa, the younger brother of Rangers hurler Ed Correa, Ramser gave the team eight demands: a $250,000 signing bonus, the right not to pitch from sundown Friday until sundown Saturday because of religious beliefs, a major league contract in his third year, an invitation to the major league camp every spring, a $75,000 bonus when he makes his major league debut, four airplane tickets for his parents per year for five years, a 1987 black Corvette for himself, and a new Cutlass Supreme for his father. The Brewers signed him without giving in to most of his demands.

Former Heisman Trophy winner Bo Jackson, whose 1987 contract with the Royals had prohibited him from playing pro football, threatened in midseason to quit the team if he couldn't sign with the Los Angeles Raiders and play in the NFL during the off-season. Royals co-owner Avron Fogelman relented and restructured Jackson's contract so he could play pro football as, Jackson said, a "hobby." This ticked off his baseball teammates, many of whom have clauses in their contracts restricting them from any sort of risky extracurricular activity. Said George Brett, "I'm thinking about taking up Brahma bull riding and sword fighting."

Brett has learned a thing or two about negotiating, including extracting an extra, unexpected concession from the front office. Recalls Lou Gorman, "When I signed George Brett, he said to me,

'Now I want you to do me one more favor before I sign the contract. I want you to sign my brother Robert too. He's an outfielder at Chapman College and he's a pretty good player.' I agreed. Robert played in the minors for about four years before we released him."

Most players use an agent because they believe he can get them more money, says John Mullen, assistant general manager of the Braves. "If I were a player, I'd get an agent. He can get you more money. It's funny, but when you're negotiating a player's contract, you deal with the agent 99 percent of the time and the player one percent until the contract is signed. Players don't feel secure in talking to the front office without their agent. They're afraid they might say something that would hurt what their agent is trying to do for them.

"On the other hand, Doyle Alexander negotiates his own contracts. The first time around with the Braves [in 1980], he had two years left in his contract at $150,000 a year. He demanded to renegotiate and we said no. Even though he would have become a free agent [in 1982], he demanded to be traded. So we traded him and that meant he lost his chance for free agency for five years."

Players still shake their heads over the negotiating skills of Derrel Thomas. In the middle of the 1985 season, the Phillies plucked the seemingly washed-up veteran out of Class-A ball in Miami and gave him a second chance as a utility player. "He did a good job for them and earned the then-minimum major league salary of $62,000," said Philadelphia beat writer Bill Brown. "They offered him $200,000 for the following year, but he turned them down and held out for a two-year contract because he said he had been treated unjustly financially during his major league career and he wanted to make it right. Eventually, the Phils took their offer off the table and he never played again."

Then there is the case of Ray Knight. After being named the MVP of the 1986 World Series, Knight rejected the Mets' offer of $800,000, became a free agent, and signed with Baltimore for only $500,000. "You ought to see my mail," he said. "I didn't know there were so many ways to call somebody stupid."

SWEETENING A DEAL WITH JELL-O

When Astros reliever Charlie Kerfeld learned that bullpen mate Jim Deshaies had signed for $110,000 in 1987, Kerfeld wanted more. Because his number was 37, Kerfeld asked for a contract of $110,037.37 plus 37 boxes of orange Jell-O. Said a member of the team, "The front office went along with it just to placate Charlie."

INCENTIVES AND BIG MONEY—DO THEY AFFECT PLAYER PERFORMANCE?

Although no player is going to turn down a chance to make as much money as he can, the *Baseball Confidential* survey revealed that many players admit big salaries and incentive bonuses can adversely affect performance:

Von Hayes, Phillies: "I've seen players on the verge of stardom get affected by big contracts. They press too much and try too hard. Incentive clauses sometimes keep players on the field when they shouldn't be. It used to be that a minor injury would take a guy out of the lineup. Now incentives keep the player going because he needs his at-bats or appearances on the mound to collect bonus money."

Hal McRae, Royals: "It was more fun when I was making $20,000 a year [in 1970]. There wasn't as much pressure even though you gave 100 percent. Now someone making $500,000 has to produce and can't make mistakes. The pressure is enormous and fans expect more from players just because they are making so much money."

Jerry Reed, Mariners: "When I was with Cleveland in 1985, we had a pitcher who had incentives in his contract. Instead of worrying about 'I have to win tonight,' he was just thinking, 'Well, this is another start and I need to go six innings.' He had figured out exactly how much he needed to do to collect his incentives. It didn't matter to him that we lost 102 games. That's the way it is with some players. The money and incentives are everything."

Atlanta Brave: "Bob Horner was so preoccupied with his big-money contract [in 1986] that it was the talk of the clubhouse. Many of the players sensed that Horner became a little too worried about his contract and not concerned enough about the team's on-the-field problems. Horner went to management repeatedly during the season to renegotiate and the club refused. Now he's got a big contract—in Japan."

Bill Brown, Philadelphia beat writer: "Some players think that teams will deliberately keep certain players out of the lineup after the pennant race is over so they don't have to pay them bonus money. Here's an example where that's not true: In 1986, [Phils reliever] Kent Tekulve's contract said that if he appeared in 70 games, his contract was automatically renewed for $800,000. He also was to receive $5,000 an appearance after 70 games. When the Phils were 21 games behind and out of the pennant race, they still brought in Tekulve, even though they could have easily brought in someone else and saved themselves money. They were still concerned about winning."

FAT BONUSES

Of all the special clauses that make it into baseball contracts, none is viewed with more scorn by players than weight clauses, according to the survey.

Several major leaguers receive a bonus if, at monthly weigh-ins, their weight is less than the limit established in their contract.

"Weight clauses are crazy," says Mike Pagliarulo of the Yankees. "A player should be in good condition to begin with." Adds teammate Lenn Sakata, "That's a great contract clause. Lose a few pounds, show up, get weighed, and collect a whole bunch of money. We should all be so fat."

WHICH OWNERS DO PLAYERS RESPECT THE MOST AND THE LEAST?

Most Respected:	*Least Respected:*
1. **Avron Fogelman, Royals**	1. **George Steinbrenner, Yankees**
2. **Bud Selig, Brewers**	2. **George Argyros, Mariners**

The man named most often in the *Baseball Confidential* survey as the most respected owner in baseball is Avron Fogelman, co-owner of the Royals—and for one main reason.

"He's given his big stars lifetime contracts," says an Indian. "Now that's an owner who takes care of his players." Fogelman gave lifetime contracts to George Brett, Willie Wilson, and Dan Quisenberry that will continue to pay the three stars long after they retire from baseball. "Every player I've talked to from the Royals says he's very happy with the organization," claims Tom Brunansky of the Twins.

Also highly respected by players is Bud Selig of the Brewers. "If players have a grievance, they can talk to him face-to-face," says Lenn Sakata of the Yankees. "He attends most every game and backs his players." Adds the Mets' Bob Gibson, who played for the Brewers from 1983–86, "Selig is very respected by his players. Everybody thinks he's fair. He's easy to talk to, fairly accessible, and seems to let the baseball people run the baseball side."

The same can hardly be said about George Steinbrenner of the Yankees, who, not surprisingly, garnered more votes for "least respected owner" than all others combined. Most of the other votes cast were for George Argyros of the Mariners.

"No matter how good things are going for the Yankees, Steinbrenner will find a way to louse it up with his insulting remarks," said a Red Sox player. For example, he pointed to Steinbrenner's criticism of Don Mattingly for hitting home runs in eight consecutive games in

1987. After Mattingly strained his wrist in the ninth game and missed a couple of games, Steinbrenner said, "Mattingly was being selfish swinging for home runs when he should have been thinking of the team."

Other players agreed that Steinbrenner's effect on the Yankees has been devastating. "In 1987, the team was in the thick of the pennant race and then George publicly got on [manager] Lou Piniella's case needlessly and the team went downhill," said a Blue Jay. Adds Tom Brunansky of the Twins, "The ex-Yankees I've talked to say they are happy to leave and the reason they always give is George."

Says Kirk Gibson of the Tigers, "George claims he's the skipper of the ship. We joke around the clubhouse that when George's ship is sinking, he's the first one off. And if that's not bad enough, he takes all the life rafts with him."

Another George—Argyros—has been following Steinbrenner's lead. "It's hard to play when the owner is constantly in the clubhouse," says Mike Smithson of the Twins. "Argyros doesn't let the baseball people run the business." Adds a National Leaguer who once played for Argyros, "He's the worst. He tries to tell the manager what to do. He doesn't have the knowledge of baseball to be that involved. He's a businessman, not a baseball man."

PAR FOR THE COURSE

Rangers' veteran utility man Tom Paciorek, who has played on six teams, says the best owner he ever met was the late Walter O'Malley of the Dodgers.

"When I was a rookie, I was playing golf at Dodgertown [the team's spring-training facility] in a foursome ahead of O'Malley's foursome," Paciorek recalls. "I was just a beginner and I lost a ball and we were looking for it. Finally, O'Malley found it and discovered I had been using a range ball. He said, 'Hey, you're not supposed to use range balls to play.' And I said, 'Gee, Mr. O'Malley, I'm sorry, but I can't afford any real good golf balls. You're not paying me enough money.'

"The next day I went to the clubhouse and there in my locker were a dozen golf balls. Walter O'Malley was a great man. I really loved him."

THE GRAND-STANDS

WHICH TEAMS HAVE THE WORST FANS?

1. **Yankees**
2. **Mets**
3. **Athletics**
4. **Giants**
5. **Phillies**

Maybe it's the way they heap abuse on both the visiting and home teams; maybe it's the way they spray the field with obscenities; maybe it's the way they harass each other in the stands. Whatever the reasons, Yankee fans are rated the worst in baseball.

"They know it and they enjoy it," declares Kirk Gibson of the Tigers. "The first two words that Yankee fans learned was 'You bum.' They they learned, 'You suck' followed by 'Gimme a ball.' If you don't give them a ball, they'll give you a complete sentence: 'You bum, you suck!' "

Throughout the league, players have complained about the nuts at Yankee Stadium who fling objects such as knives, bottles, and golf balls at the players. "When you get stuff thrown at you and have beer dumped on you like I have, that tends to sway your opinion," says Blue Jays reliever Tom Henke. "I bet you can't find too many ballplayers who enjoy playing there."

Certainly not among the Red Sox. "Some fans at Yankee Stadium nearly caused a riot a couple of years ago," recalled Boston's Rich Gedman. "Someone went after [left fielder] Jim Rice and stole his hat, so Jim went after him in the stands and about 10 of us followed him. You take your life in your hands when you go into the stands at Yankee Stadium. But we had to protect our teammate."

Players feel they have to protect their families there as well. "There are so many fights breaking out there that I told my wife and kids not to come to the games," said the Angels' Butch Wynegar, who played four years for the Yankees. "The fans can just brutally abuse you and they have no respect at all for anybody."

Not even toward their own players. That's because the fans have short memories, says Dan Plesac of the Brewers. "There was a game this season when the Yankees' best reliever, Dave Righetti, came in to pitch the ninth inning against us in New York. The fans were on their feet cheering him. After all, the year before he set a record for most saves with 46. But in the game against us, he gave up a homer and they turned on him in an instant, booing him like crazy. Then he gave up another homer and it was like he was the worst pitcher in the world. They booed him right out of the stadium and that was kind of a shock to see."

It's no more surprising than what happens a few miles away at Shea Stadium. "Mets fans are just too abusive toward their own players let alone the opposing players," said a New York player. In 1987, Mets reliever Doug Sisk was booed so unmercifully by the Shea fans that he says, "I won't even let my wife come to the games anymore at home." Met fans have thrown ice at Sisk in the on-deck circle and scratched the hood of his new Mercedes. Former Met Ray Knight, now with the Orioles, says New Yorkers can be the best fans in the world—as long as the team is winning. But heaven help you if you or the team should falter. "When we were on the way to the world championship in 1986, fans catered to us. There was no place I went that I had to pay for dinner. But whenever the team does poorly, they are on you unmercifully. They are relentless."

A couple of players have put forth theories to explain this outrageous behavior. "Met fans are definitely taking their aggressions out at the ball park," says Bryn Smith of the Expos. Kent Tekulve of the Phillies believes that Met fans "have an image to live up to—which happens to be rowdy, raunchy, and ridiculous."

Mark Grant of the Padres can't get over how rude they are. "They don't say please or anything nice. They demand things like, 'Sign my ball' or 'Give me an autograph.' One time a guy shouted at me, 'Hey, give me a ball.' I said, 'No, I can't.' And he said, 'Well fuck you, you fucking fuck!' as loud as he could in front of children and everybody."

Fans aren't any better in San Francisco and Oakland, according to the *Baseball Confidential* survey. "They're rotten," declares Kent Hrbek of the Twins. "They're on you all the time and they don't have any respect for other people who are trying to watch the game."

At the Oakland Coliseum, fans bombard visiting players with a constant barrage of verbal garbage. "You hear them no matter where you are on the field," says Mark Gubicza of the Royals. "One guy sits right by the runway going to the clubhouse and he gets on me every single game."

One of the players whom Athletics fans love to hate is Kirk Gibson of the Tigers. "They target not only me, but my mother, my wife, my grandmother, my city, my IQ. I think they pass a sheet of paper out at the beginning of the year so they can memorize 20 nasty things to say to ballplayers. You hear the same kind of thing every inning. One guy will stand up and shout, 'What's the matter with Gibson?' And then 50 people will stand up and yell, 'He's a bum!' It's all orchestrated. They know that we players hear them. I don't think they're the real career-oriented type of people out there because they're always there at night and during the day. I wonder what these people do for a living because they never seem to be working."

When Cubs' reliever Ron Davis was with the Twins in 1986, he always found a safe haven in the dugout at the Oakland Coliseum. He claimed there were so many marijuana smokers in the seats near the bullpen that he wouldn't go out to the pen until the seventh inning. "Otherwise I could test positive just from breathing the air in the bullpen."

Across the Bay in Candlestick Park, Giants fans continue to fight for the league lead in disturbances. Their main target: the archrival Dodgers. Early in the 1987 season, fans near the Dodger dugout launched a salvo of beer, soft drinks, and oranges at Los Angeles players. Not even a dozen of the city's finest who stood guard in front of the visitors' dugout could halt the bombardment. Recalls former Dodger Dave Stewart, now with the Athletics, "I'll never forget the time in San Francisco when we had to be escorted off the field by a circle of police. We hadn't been in a fight with the Giants or anything. All we did was win a game yet we had to have police protect us from the fans."

During the 1987 National League Championship Series, Giants fans showed a national TV audience why players consider them so bad. They tossed rolls of toilet paper and beachballs at the Cardinals and threw cookies to rotund umpire Eric Gregg. "These fans have a reputation to uphold and they're very proud of it," Giants catcher

Bob Brenly told the press. "They've worked hard to be some of the most hated fans in the league."

At least fans in the Bay Area vent their spleen at the visitors. Phillies fans spew most of their venom on the home team. "They're so hard on their own team that they harass not only the players but the *families* of players," says a Yankee who's a former National Leaguer. "Now that's bad, brother."

Roger McDowell of the Mets says he feels sorry for the big-name Phillies who must subject themselves to needless harassment. "It's not right that a superstar like Mike Schmidt gets booed. And look what happened to Lance Parrish after he came over from Detroit. The fans expected him to hit 50 homers and drive in 150 RBIs, and when he couldn't, they got on him terribly." The fans were so mean to Parrish that to spare his family further grief he sent them home to California before the All-Star break.

Several American Leaguers felt dishonorable mention should go to the Tigers fans. "They're good for the home team but they are the worst for visiting teams," says Ron Washington of the Orioles. "The fans there make so much noise that they can scare you." Lloyd Moseby of the Blue Jays says that when Tiger Stadium is full of screaming fans, it's deafening for the players. "It's the most intimidating thing a player can experience because you can't hear your teammate and can't communicate with each other."

Many players feel the Pittsburgh fans deserve a round of boos for their horrendous lack of support. "The Pirates have a number of good, young players," says Charlie Kerfeld of the Astros. "The team could use encouragement, yet only 4,000 fans ever show up to see them play."

Cleveland fans received a few votes for turning their backs on the Indians. Says Pete Incaviglia of the Rangers, "There aren't that many fans there. But the few who show up are rough. When I'm in left field, I get called every name in the book."

Even though Cubs fans are considered among the best in baseball, Mark Grant of the Padres has a gripe about them. "They throw beer on you in the outfield. If they're going to do that, the least they can do is throw it in a cup so you can get a chance to drink it."

SILENCING THE CALL OF THE BOO-BIRD

Veteran reliever Aurelio Lopez offers this advice to players who want to shut up the boo-birds:

"I always stop at the top of the dugout and allow them to really let loose. But the moment I look up, it stops. Suddenly people aren't so brave when you look right at them."

WHICH TEAMS HAVE THE BEST FANS?

1. **Cubs**
2. **Cardinals**
3. **Royals**
4. **Dodgers**

Playing on the road doesn't necessarily mean the visiting team will face a hostile crowd. In some cities, fans treat opposing clubs with the civility and appreciation usually given only to the home team.

Whether they want to admit it or not, most players hear the cheers and the boos. And on the road, they're likely to hear more boos than cheers. That's all the more reason why players don't forget the cities where fans applaud them for good plays and joke around with them.

"The mood at Wrigley Field is like none other," says journeyman Tom Paciorek. "It's like a carnival atmosphere. The fans really enjoy the game and they stay for the final out. You won't find more vocal fans anywhere."

What strikes players most about Cub fans is the unique way opponents are treated. "It's a strange thing," said a Reds player. "The fans at Wrigley Field will get on you unbelievably. Yet if you make a great play, they cheer their asses off. They appreciate good performances."

They also appreciate players with a sense of humor. "I love going to Chicago," says Roger McDowell of the Mets. "I get along well with the fans, especially the Bleacher Bums. During BP, I play catch with them. But sometimes I'll throw a ball to them and they won't throw it back."

According to the players, the most well-behaved fans reside in St. Louis. "They come out and root for their team without giving the other team a hard time," says Kent Tekulve of the Phillies. "They aren't rowdy." During his stint in the National League, Pat Clements of the Yankees noticed that Cardinal fans create "a family-type atmosphere that's great for baseball." Not only that but "they are the cleanest, best-dressed fans in the majors," claims Pirates coach Ray Miller. "They look like they took a shower and put on their best casual clothes before coming to the ball park." (The fans' only black mark came during the 1987 National League Championship Series when a very small group of unruly fans threw cow bells and beer at Giants outfielder Jeffrey Leonard.)

Admiring Cardinal fans go out of their way to meet the players from other teams. "They show up at our team hotel, across the street from the ball park, and just mill around for hours before and after the game," said a Houston Astro. "They don't do it only when we're in town. They do that with all the visiting teams."

On the other side of Missouri, Royals fans get top marks for the respect they show visitors. That makes their idol, George Brett, proud. "It feels good when other players come up to me and say we have the most polite fans in baseball." In stark contrast to many other parks, "You never hear insults and booing toward opponents in Kansas City," says Floyd Rayford of the Orioles.

The same holds true for Dodger fans. "When I go on the road, I think about the fans who rag on me, yet Dodger Stadium is one place where fans don't rag the visiting players," says the White Sox's Gary Redus, a former National Leaguer. Fans there want to see a good game and they recognize talent in all uniforms, adds another former National Leaguer, Mike Easler of the Yankees. "The stadium there is always full and it's a lot more fun to play in front of a big crowd." With some twisted logic, an All-Star hurler explains why he thinks Dodger fans are the best: "They leave in the seventh inning, so you never have trouble getting out of the parking lot after the game."

A TOUCHING STORY

In the middle of some idle chitchat at first base with Pirates runner Jim Morrison during a 1987 game in Pittsburgh, Mets first baseman Keith Hernandez was startled to see a young woman approach him. Recalled Hernandez, "She said, 'I'll give you 20 dollars if I can touch you.' Before I could say, 'Make it 100 dollars,' she touched me."

 ## WHICH TEAMS HAVE THE MOST AND LEAST KNOWLEDGEABLE FANS?

Most:	*Least:*
1. **Red Sox**	1. **Blue Jays**
2. **Cardinals**	2. **Expos**
3. **Mets and**	3. **Mariners**
Yankees	
(tie)	

If you want to talk baseball with fans in the know, go to Boston, St. Louis, or New York. Players believe the fans in those cities possess the most baseball smarts.

"The Red Sox fans are the most knowledgeable," contends Jamie Quirk of the Royals. "They know who every man on the team is and what his role is. They know the strengths and weaknesses of the opposing players too."

They know who's hurt and appreciate the gamers who play with pain. For example, several players cited a game in 1987 involving Boston's Bill Buckner, who was in pain from injured ankles. On a 3–2 pitch to teammate Don Baylor, Buckner tried to steal second base four times on those wobbly ankles, but each time Buckner broke for second, Baylor fouled off the pitch. "Each time the fans gave an incredible applause to Buckner for this gutsy effort," said an Athletic. "In most cities, that would have slipped by the fans."

Cardinal fans are much like Boston's, according to the *Baseball Confidential* survey. "Cardinal fans know strategy," says Pirates coach Ray Miller. "They appreciate the finer points. If the Cards have a runner on second with no outs and the next batter hits a grounder to the right side to advance the runner, they cheer. Fans don't do that in most other parks. They boo the batter for making an out."

There's a downside to playing in front of knowledgeable fans—they can be very demanding, as any Yankee or Met will attest. "New York fans know their baseball, and if you don't perform, they get on you real fast," says Mike Easler of the Yankees. Adds former Met Ray Knight, now of the Orioles, "They know what it takes to win, and if you don't win, they are relentless. They don't let up."

Teams don't have that problem in Canada, probably because players consider the fans in Toronto and Montreal the least knowledgeable about baseball. That might be a little unfair, considering fans in St. Louis, Boston, and New York have had more than 80 years to watch major league baseball while Canadians have had less than 20.

"Blue Jay fans are out of the game," says Bobby Meacham of the Yankees. "They don't cheer or boo very much. They just sit there and wait to see what happens. If the scoreboard shows the Blue Jays scored a run, then the fans cheer."

It's the same in Montreal, says a Houston Astro. "The fans there just don't understand the game. They're really lost. It could be the eighth inning with the tying run on first and no outs and they can't understand why the batter is bunting. They really have no idea what's going on."

Neither do the Mariner fans, according to American Leaguers. "How can they learn the game?" asks Ron Washington of the Orioles. "There's never anyone in the stands."

WHICH TEAMS HAVE THE FOXIEST FANS?

1. **Angels**
2. **Dodgers**
3. **Padres**
4. **Cubs**
5. **Rangers**

Players have been know to check out the stands for pretty girls. To be honest, they don't just look; they ogle—before, during, and after games. As a result, players have developed a certain expertise when it comes to judging beautiful fans.

Wallace Johnson of the Expos says that during lulls in the game, he scans the crowd for pretty girls. "You don't always think about baseball during the game. Sometimes you look at the chicks sitting in the third-base box seats. You can't help it. The trouble is it can really break your concentration, especially in San Diego. That's a bikini-type crowd during day games."

According to the *Baseball Confidential* survey, San Diego, Los Angeles, and Anaheim possess more "10's" than the other big league cities. "Without a doubt, southern California has the nicest-looking women," says Dan Plesac of the Brewers, echoing the voices of a majority of the surveyed players. "Anaheim is the best. There aren't just one or two beautiful women. There are thousands. It's like a breeding ground." What Kent Hrbek of the Twins says he enjoys most about Anaheim Stadium is that "wherever you look, there are halter tops floating around."

An Angels player claims that even though foxy fans adorn Anaheim Stadium, "the girls in Arlington, Texas, are knockouts. They go out of their way to dress up for ball games."

Maybe so, but players want to see less clothes and more skin. During the summer, you can't beat Wrigley Field for girl-watching, says Bryn Smith of the Expos. "They play day games there so it gets hot and that means lots of halter tops and bikinis." Adds a married

Phillies player, who can look but not touch, "You should be fined if you go to Wrigley Field without binoculars."

After spending 12 years in the National League, including over a year with the Dodgers, Bill Madlock of the Tigers says he's never seen sexier fans than the ones in Los Angeles. He believes there's something about Dodger Stadium that seems to trigger a player's innate awareness of where the most seductive fans sit. "It's amazing," says Madlock. "There could be 50,000 people at Dodger Stadium during a game and a girl will bare her breasts and all nine of us out on the field will look in the stands at the same time and see her do it without having to tell each other."

To make girl-watching easier for players, Madlock has a suggestion. "There should be a special section for fans in halter tops, so we don't have to scope the whole stadium. That way, we can concentrate on only one part of the stands."

WHAT RUSES DO PLAYERS USE TO AVOID SIGNING AUTOGRAPHS?

Day in and day out, major league ballplayers are besieged with requests for autographs. Fans crowd around players at the clubhouse entrance, mob them in hotel lobbies, and interrupt their dinner in restaurants. Some players handle it well; others don't.

"People think that because we are ballplayers, we are obligated to sign autographs and talk to them," says Kent Tekulve of the Phillies. "Our obligation to fans is to give them a good baseball game. I'm a firm believer in signing autographs, but there are some occasions when I just don't want to sign because I have something important to do or have to be somewhere at a certain time. Even though I may have spent 50 nights in a row signing autographs after the game, all of a sudden if I say no, I'm the worst guy on the face of the earth. That upsets me."

Rick Manning of the Brewers wishes fans understood the players' side more. "A lot of times after a long day, I don't feel like signing autographs. I sign before the game, but after spending six or seven hours at the ball park, I want to get home and relax. When I leave the park, I try to be honest with the fans. I tell them, 'No, not right now.' I know some people get mad, but I can't help that."

When players don't want to sign, they resort to some tricks of the trade. Steve Lombardozzi of the Twins relies on two popular ploys. "I wait until one of the big stars is leaving the clubhouse entrance and I walk behind him and yell something like 'There's Kirby Puckett!' All the kids run to him and then I can slide right by him. Or I have my wife come to the clubhouse with our 14-month-old baby. I'll carry the baby in my arms and walk past the hundreds of kids to my car. They don't bother me because they can see that I can't sign."

The old my-hands-are-full trick has worked for years for several Yankees who often carry a drink in one hand and a briefcase in the other when they leave the park. Teammates claim Larry Parrish of the Rangers once wore an ice pack on his right hand to avoid signing as he walked to his car.

"Sometimes it's hard," says a Yankee. "If you stop for one, you'll be surrounded by 50. By the time you reach your car, you have pencil and pen marks all over your clothes."

Roger Clemens of the Red Sox says he tries to sign as many as he can, but not on getaway days. "We have to wear suits or sports jackets when we travel and I've had three jackets ruined by fans with their sharp pens. So on getaway days, I just tell the kids, 'Send a card to Fenway Park and I'll mail it back.' "

Kevin Gross of the Phillies does what many players are forced to do—sign on the run. "You have to push through the crowd and say you're in a hurry if you ever want to get to your car." Other players try to sneak out side entrances or, when possible, have their wives drive right up to the clubhouse door.

On the field, players who are reluctant to sign simply ignore the fans' pleas. Says Don Carman of the Phillies, "If I don't feel like signing that day, I tell the fans, 'I'll get you after BP.' Then at the end of BP, I jog by the fans as if I have to get to the clubhouse in a hurry."

What bothers players the most are the autograph seekers who pursue them away from the ball park—in restaurants or hotel lobbies. The majority of players will not sign in the middle of a meal. "Give me a break," said an All-Star. "I just want to eat in privacy without having a pen shoved in my face. Where are their manners?"

Fans lie in wait in lobbies, hounding stars to give them autographs or pose for photos. "I'll sign at the ball park," says Tim Flannery of the Padres, "but not in hotels. I don't sign autographs at my house and I won't in hotels because that's my home away from home."

Because superstars make no more than nine appearances a year in any one city on the road, they are badgered by autograph seekers with even greater fervor. To make matters worse on the road, the stars are also more exposed to the public because they live in hotels and eat in restaurants. "If Mike Schmidt stops to sign autographs after the game, he'll never get to the hotel," says Philadelphia beat writer Bill Brown. "In St. Louis, we used to stay at the Marriott right across the street from the stadium because it was so convenient. But there was always a mob scene in the lobby and on the sidewalk to the stadium. So Schmitty used to leave by a back door of the hotel, walk several blocks out of his way, and then enter through a back gate of the stadium just to avoid the mob of autograph seekers." Since the Braves stay at that hotel, Dale Murphy must take a similar pregame journey to the park.

Under the proper circumstances, most players don't mind signing autographs for fans. But there are those moments when stars wonder what it would be like to walk in public without being asked, "Sign this." Muses George Brett, "When I see other guys not even get stopped, I say to myself, 'That must be fun to walk out, be ignored, and walk right to your car and go on your way.' Instead, you walk out and people are yelling, 'Sign this! Sign this!' My father has told me this many times: 'When they quit asking for your autograph, you're going to miss it.' I say, 'Well, let me find that out for myself. I don't think I'll miss it.'"

SUIT YOURSELF

While signing autographs near the stands in Kansas City in 1985, Lance Parrish, then with the Tigers, was flipped a piece of paper. He picked it up and found it was a summons concerning a minor suit he was involved in.

WHY YOU CAN'T BLAME PLAYERS FOR SAYING NO TO AUTOGRAPH HOUNDS

Most players don't mind signing autographs. Many actually enjoy it. But almost every player has a horror story to tell of an obnoxious, rude, or mean fan whose actions give autograph seekers a bad name. Some examples:

George Brett, Royals: "One time, someone asked me to sign a piece of paper and I did. Then he ripped it up in front of my face. It makes you wonder. . . ."

Mike Boddicker, Orioles: "I was signing autographs for a good 20 minutes after the game when I had to cut it off because I had company waiting for me at home. As I got into my car, this little old lady—she had to be at least 70—came up to me, flipped me off, and told me, 'You're a fucking asshole!' It caught me by such a surprise that I started laughing. I laughed about it the whole way home."

Paul Mirabella, Brewers: "I got an earful of obscenities when I turned down a request from a fan during batting practice at Yankee Stadium. The swear words weren't from some adult but an eight-year-old kid. He was giving me the finger and cursing me. And would you believe it? His father was cheering him on! I stood there and shook my head and wondered what kind of a person this kid was going to be when he grew up."

Mel Stottlemyre, Mets coach: "I've heard a few blue words in my baseball career, but the foulest mouth I ever heard came from a grade school autograph seeker. I wanted to find his parents and choke them."

Gary Redus, White Sox: "My worst experience with an autograph hound happened when I played for the Reds. I had been signing for several minutes after a game in Cincinnati when I told the crowd, 'I've got to go now.' This one guy said, 'Hey, we're paying your salary.' And I told him, 'Hey, I never saw your name on my check.' He got mad and tried to block my car. We almost got into a fight."

Roger Clemens, Red Sox: "I don't know whether it's a phobia or what, but I have a hard time dealing with a lot of people around me at one time. I don't know these people. I will try and honor their requests for autographs, but sometimes they get too aggressive. I've been in situations when my family is with me and the crowd gets pushy while asking for my autograph. If my family should get hurt by autograph seekers, then I'm either going to hurt somebody or go berserk. The other night, a grown man threw a 13-year-old kid out of the way to get my autograph. That's when I say no more autographs. That's where I draw the line."

Tim Flannery, Padres: "Some fans will follow you everywhere, even into your hotel. I can remember seeing a fan with a video camera filming Steve Garvey as he went from the lobby and up the elevator to his room. They'll knock on your door or call you on the house phone and lie to you just to get you to come down and sign something."

Gary Lucas, Angels: "I wish parents wouldn't let their children hang out all day in hotel lobbies where they ambush players for autographs. After a long night game we'll get back to the hotel around midnight and see all these little 10-year-olds waiting in the lobby with their parents urging them on."

Tom Henke, Blue Jays: "I don't like the fan who comes up to you with 12 cards and wants you to sign them all."

Mike Easler, Yankees: "The most bizarre request I've ever had was when a sexy lady asked me to autograph her chest. I said, 'No way, Jose!' "

Phil Niekro, Indians: "One fan wrote me a two-page letter as nice as could be. At the bottom, he said, 'Please sign your autograph. If you don't, go to hell!' "

WHAT QUESTIONS WOULD YOU LIKE TO ASK A MAJOR LEAGUER?

Do you have a question about baseball that you wish ballplayers would answer for you? Perhaps we can include it in a future survey of major leaguers. If you have any questions on baseball—or any other sport—that you think belong in a survey, please jot them down and sent them to us at:

Nash & Zullo Productions
P. O. Box 31867
Palm Beach Gardens, FL 33410